I0485908

WORK BENEFITS IN AMERICA:

A SOCIETAL PERSPECTIVE

Robert Klonoski, JD, DMgt

Copyright © 2015 Robert Klonoski

All rights reserved.

ISBN: 1516962664
ISBN-13: 978-1516962662

DEDICATION

To my wife Grace whose help and advice
made this work possible.

CONTENTS

PREFACE

This work began with a study of work motivation, but as researchers will often say, the process of discovery is seldom linear. How we feel about work and how we respond to it is shaped by our internal motivations as much as it is by the environment of the workplace. Every workplace has its own internal culture, a combination of the personalities of the people who participate in it and the shared experiences they have had. But organizations also exist in a broader cultural context and are a reflection of societal values.

There is a case to be made for the social protection of the aged, the ill, the young, the parents of minor children as well as for workers in general. There is an equal case to be made for giving people a chance to reap the benefits of their individual labors, for giving them the opportunity to negotiate their own terms of work and compensation. Over time, in the U.S. as well as in other countries, social protections for the elderly, for parents, for the ill, and for others with deserving circumstances have been gaining ground. Many countries have passed laws that ensure that workers will have some form of social security payments upon their retirement and that they will have access to subsidized health care whether it is financed by their employers or their governments, that they will have paid time off, and more.

The U.S. has been slower than most countries to adopt these sorts of measures. Certainly no one would like to see the U.S. return to the early days of capitalism, to child labor, unsafe working conditions, monopolies and robber barons. Going forward, the question becomes one of the extent to which we are willing to accept regulation, to determine whether it is needed and under what circumstances, and then to determine exactly what form the regulation should take.

The benefits that attach to the workplace provide a good basis for this debate. When benefits are awarded, they are done so for all full time employees. Some, such as health insurance, are generally available to all at the same level; others, such as time off, may depend on rank or tenure with the organization. These are shared resources, a common bond among employees and something that, at the lower and middle management levels of an organization are rarely negotiated for individual employees.

Some readers may find it surprising how few benefits in the U.S. (versus most other countries) are regulated or a mandatory part of an employment contract. Those most affected by this are generally the lower wage level employees in small establishments in the service trades.

The case for social protection is compelling, as is the case for individual freedoms. Does social protection enhance or inhibit the development of human capital? Does it promote or inhibit economic development? Does it help or hinder our social and economic environments?

ACKNOWLEDGMENTS

I wish to thank Dr. Joanne Tritsch for reviewing parts of this manuscript. I also wish to express my gratitude to my colleagues in the Business Faculty at Mary Baldwin College for their ideas and suggestions in compiling this work, and to thank the Society for Human Resource Management, the International Labour Organization and the Organisation for Economic Co-operation and Development for the outstanding bodies of research they have complied on this very important topic.

1 INTRODUCTION

"Works and days were offered us, and we took works."

Ralph Waldo Emerson
Society and Solitude: Twelve Chapters (1857)

Background

Work benefits are any form of indirect or non-cash compensation paid to an employee. They may be required by law, such as employer contributions to Social Security, unemployment compensation or worker's compensation, or they may be discretionary, such as retirement, paid time off or family-friendly benefits. They are provided to employees to boost their loyalty and increase their job satisfaction.

Work benefits can take many forms. In 2014, in its annual report on employee benefits[1], the Society for Human Resource Management listed more than 300 specific types of benefits that organizations offer their employees ranging from healthcare subsidies to take your pet to work days. Some benefits pertain only to those who rank at the top of their organizations. University presidents are usually offered on-campus housing; chief executive officers of large corporations may have use of private jets for their business travel. While the number of available benefits is great and executive perks would perhaps make an interesting study of its own, this book addresses only the most common categories of benefits -- those that are widely available to employees and middle management in the United States.

The categories of benefits that are studied here include retirement, time off, healthcare, family and medical leave, and flexible work arrangements - the categories of benefits and scheduling options that are most frequently offered by organizations. Each of these categories has a unique history and path of development. They are products of market demand and of public policy and are influenced by changes in demographics, by trends in cultural development and by short and longer term shifts in the economy. There is a chapter discussing some of the environmental influences (cultural, regulatory and economic) on work benefits. This is followed by a series of chapters dedicated to each of the major categories of benefits - tracing their histories and outlining some of the more critical issues surrounding them, and, where possible, showing how benefits are treated in other countries.

For purposes of international comparisons, data was taken from the International Labour Organization (ILO) and the Organisation for Economic Co-operation and Development (OECD). The ILO was founded in 1919, as part of the Treaty of Versailles that ended World War I and became the first specialized agency of the United Nations in 1946. The organization researches and reports on employment and job quality, social security, and labor standards along with many other related topics. The OECD was founded in 1960 and began with eighteen European countries, the U.S. and Canada, but has since grown to include thirty-four of the world's most advanced economies along with several emerging countries. The organization provides research on topics including employment and the quality of jobs, returns on investment in social security, inequality, instability and employment, and international labour standards.

Historical Context of Work Benefits

Why should an employer provide anything to an employee other than a monetary compensation? The origins of work benefits can be found in many places and cultures, but for the set of work benefits with which Americans are familiar, a turning point in history took place in Germany in the late 1800s.

In the mid-19th century, Germany was a fragmented country, split into four kingdoms, twelve duchies, twelve principalities and three free cities. In 1862, King Wilhelm I promoted Otto von Bismarck to the position of Minister President of Prussia. Under Bismarck's direction a united Germany was formed and in 1871 he was appointed its first Chancellor. The new country began to industrialize; its population grew rapidly and moved to urban centers. In the two decades following 1871, Berlin doubled in population from one to two million people and cities in the Ruhr region, the upper Rhine Valley, the Neckar Valley and Saxony tripled or quadrupled in size[2].

The country's legislature, the Reichstag, had representatives from six political parties: the Conservative Party, the Free Conservative Party, the National Liberal Party, the Progressive Party, the Center Party, and the Social Democratic Party of Germany (Sozialdemokratische Partei Deutschlands – SPD). This diverse set of parties represented each of Germany's main constituent interests: the aristocracy and landed gentry, the industrialists and large commercial interests (the group with whom Bismarck was most closely aligned), the liberals, the Catholic minority who supported the monarchy but were interested in social reform, and the Socialists. Of these groups, it was the Socialists (the SPD) who most avidly pressed for labor rights, including benefits such as health care and old age pensions[3].

The SPD was a political party that Bismarck worked to limit and suppress, in part because it advocated for a classless society with state socialism. While the SPD was willing to work through the parliamentary system to attain these ends, the Party also thought that revolution was an acceptable means for achieving its purpose. At the same time Bismarck attacked the SPD with a series of anti-socialist laws, he established national health insurance and old-age pensions, operating on the assumption that if the government protected the working class, there would be little need for a revolution. The SPD worked within the parliamentary system and after

Bismarck's dismissal from office in 1890, it continued to grow in popularity and representation in the Reichstag[4].

Socialism in the United States

In the United States, there were two related groups that advocated for the working class. One was the American Socialist Party and the other was the labor unions. In 1892, Eugene Debs founded the American Railway Union, and a mere two years later, the Pullman Company put the Union to the test. The Company cut worker pay and nearly four thousand workers went on strike, but to little effect. When the Company refused to negotiate with or even recognize the Union, Debs called for a boycott of all trains that used a Pullman car. Violence erupted, trains were disrupted, and the Company suffered significant damages. President Grover Cleveland ordered the army to stop the disruptions. The American Railway Union was dissolved; Eugene Debs was convicted of violating a court order and was sentenced to six months in prision[5].

After his jail term, Debs became a politician and in 1901 formed the Socialist Party. He ran for President five times, garnering approximately 900,000 votes in 1912 (approximately six percent of the popular vote). He protested America's involvement in World War I, was arrested and jailed for anti-war activities, and ran for President in 1920 while in jail. This time, he earned 919,000 votes – or a little more than three percent of the popular vote. The Socialist Party platform in 1912 included a number of demands advocating collective ownership of certain industries, unemployment assistance, and political reforms, but it also included ten "industrial demands." These demands were as listed as[6]:

The conservation of human resources, particularly of the lives and well-being of the workers and their families:
- By shortening the work day in keeping with the increased productiveness of machinery.
- By securing for every worker a rest period of not less than a day and a half in each week.
- By securing a more effective inspection of workshops, factories and mines.

- By the forbidding the employment of children under sixteen years of age.
- By the co-operative organization of the industries in the federal penitentiaries for the benefit of the convicts and their dependents.
- By forbidding the interstate transportation of the products of child labor, of convict labor and of all uninspected factories and mines.
- By abolishing the profit system in government work and substituting either the direct hire of labor or the awarding of contracts to co-operative groups of workers.
- By establishing minimum wage scales.
- By abolishing official charity and substituting a non-contributory system of old age pensions, a general system of insurance by the State of all its members against unemployment and invalidism and a system of compulsory insurance by employers of their workers, without cost to the latter, against industrial diseases, accidents and death.

While most of these propositions would eventually work their way into the American economic and political systems, they represented a clear departure from the capitalist view that the government should not interfere with the right of management and labor to agree on their own terms of employment. Socialism itself is an economic and political theory that advocates for community ownership of the production, distribution, and exchange of goods and services. The propositions listed above were a part of the Socialist platform of the time, but do not on their own constitute a Socialist system, rather, they establish the nation's government as being an advocate for the protection of its citizens in the workplace.

Early Union Formation

At the same time, labor had begun to organize into unions in order to improve the bargaining power of workers in their negotiations with employers. Small groups of cooperatives in trades such as tailors, shoemakers and hatters began to form unions as early as the 1830s and 40s[7]. In the aftermath of the Civil War, larger organizations began to form including the National Labor Union, the Knights of Labor, and the Federation of Organized Trades and Labor Unions (the fore-runner of the

American Federation of Labor which formed in 1881). At the beginning of the 20th century, these organizations took up a number of worker causes including the creation of cooperatives[8], worker education[9], profit sharing[10], and, perhaps the single most popular rallying point of the unions, limits on workday hours[11].

By the 1920s, the unions had made much progress in limiting the factory workday and had begun to take interest in establishing benefits such as paid time off, healthcare and retirement plans. In spite of the early victory with workday time limits, efforts to expand the list of work benefits began to stagnate. International events contributed to this. The Russian revolution of 1917 was unsettling news to the American public and the actions of the unions in organizing protests and strikes was seen as a step toward anarchism. Unions, especially the Industrial Workers of the World (IWW), opposed U.S. involvement in the First World War.

The government sought to limit this threat. Congress passed the Espionage Act of 1917 making it a crime to impede the success of the military through, for example, a disruptive strike[12]. The Sedition Act of 1918 made it a crime to "willfully utter, print, write, or publish any disloyal, profane, scurrilous, or abusive language about the form of the Government of the United States" or to "willfully urge, incite, or advocate any curtailment of the production" of the things "necessary or essential to the prosecution of the war.[13]" As for unions, in 1920, U.S. Attorney General A. Mitchell Palmer urged the deportation of "agitators who oppose the limitations of unionism"[14], and in 1921, President Warren Harding in his first Annual Message to Congress recognized the right of labor to organize and negotiate, but urged that their actions be limited by "regulations, restrictions, and in some cases detailed supervision[15]."

While the Socialist minority of union membership was vocal and garnered much public attention, most union members were more interested in steady and well-paid work than they were in social revolution or disrupting the war effort. The issues they brought to work councils and union leadership were largely limited to discipline, grievances, wages and hours and working conditions[16]. Nonetheless, the association of union membership with Socialist or Communist leanings would linger for decades.

The Great Depression to the Second World War

The Great Depression began with the stock market crash in October of 1929 and lasted well through the 1930s. With unemployment among the non-farm labor force reaching 35 percent in 1933[17], work itself rather than enterprise ownership was the critical issue of the era. Within a few years of the onset of the Depression, it became clear that the economy was not going to rebound quickly without intervention and so the federal government took unprecedented action in stimulating job growth and providing worker protections.

In 1933, the Roosevelt administration began putting programs into place as part of the "New Deal" to alleviate high unemployment, to protect small businesses, encourage union membership and provide aid to impoverished families. Federal programs including the Civil Works Administration (1933), the Civilian Conservation Corps (1933), the National Youth Administration (1935), the Public Works Administration (1933), and the Works Progress Administration (1935) all hired the unemployed to perform reforestation and conservation tasks, as well as to construct public works and to undertake projects in the arts, theatre and literature. The Wagner Act of 1935 facilitated the formation of unions and prohibited union-busting tactics by management. The National Industrial Recovery Act of 1933 permitted the collective bargaining of workers and established minimum wages. The Federal Emergency Relief Act of 1933 gave direct aid to unemployed workers, and the Social Security Act of 1935 provided retirement assistance, unemployment insurance, and aid to blind, deaf, or disabled workers and their dependent children[18]. In 1938, the Fair Labor Standards Act banned child labor and set the standard hours of work for adults at 44, a number that was revised to 40 in a 1940 amendment to the Act[19]. In sum, "New Deal" legislation addressed many of the industrial concerns that Socialists had raised 34 years earlier.

The Second World War was a turning point in making work benefits widely available. Fearful of high rates of inflation, Congress passed the Emergency Stabilization Act in October of 1942 which sought to freeze wage and salary levels[20]. As labor was in short supply, industries were pressed to attract the few available laborers who were not taken by the war effort. Companies reached out to females, a non-traditional source of employees. While organizations were not able to negotiate wages and salaries, work benefits were exempted from the wage and salary ceiling calculations imposed by the Act, and so pensions, health insurance, and paid time off became bargaining tools for attracting employees. (Later, in 1949, the Supreme Court would rule that benefits were, in fact, a part of wages and so beginning in the 1950s, benefits came under the stewardship of the National Labor Relations Board[21].) The market for benefits grew quickly. In 1940, there were approximately 21 million people in the U.S. who were enrolled in health insurance plans, by 1950 that number had grown to 142 million[22].

While the Wagner Act of 1935 had done much to support the growth of unions, the scarcity of workers during the Second World War had given labor an advantage in negotiations with employers. Unions were using tactics that went beyond mere collective bargaining and Congress acted to restrain them. In 1947, Congress passed the Labor Management Relations Act, also known as the Taft-Hartley Act. The Act made certain union practices illegal: Jurisdictional strikes – strikes called to ensure that only union workers would be assigned to particular tasks; Wildcat strikes – strikes undertaken without the consent of union leadership; Solidarity strikes – strikes undertaken by unions in companies other than the one with which a union had a grievance in order to show support for the striking union and bring peer pressure on the original company; Closed shops – where companies are required to hire union members only; and monetary donations by unions to federal political campaigns[23].

Benefits became a union cause partly as an unintended consequence of the passage of the Taft-Hartley Act. The Act had challenged the existence of unions; in response, unions found a rallying point. Bolstered by the use of benefits as a way of attracting employees during World War II, unions made work benefits a central focus of their negotiations with employers[24]. At the same time, a ruling by the Internal Revenue Service made employer contributions to health and pension benefits tax deductible business expenses. The availability of work benefits began to surge in part because unions had made a point of negotiating for them and because the federal government endorsed their use through favorable tax policies.

In the longer term, however, unions did not fare well. Membership in unions in private industry peaked in the 1950s at approximately 35 percent of the workforce[25]; by 1983, that number had fallen to approximately 20 percent and to 11 percent by 2014[26]. Because of this decline, unions have become less able to set a national agenda for work benefits.

Recent Trends in Work Benefits and the Labor Market

Congress has not acted to establish mandatory requirements for paid time off and retirement, but the Affordable Care Act of 2010 makes it mandatory for larger firms to offer healthcare benefits to all employees. Also, while the Family and Medical Leave Act of 1993 requires that 12 weeks of leave be given (on request) to new parents and for other family medical emergencies. The leave is unpaid rather than paid.

Table 1

Access to Selected Benefits, 2014 versus 1984
Establishments with 100 or More Workers
Percent of Civilian Labor Force

	1984	2014	Difference
Retirement benefits	82	85	+3
Healthcare benefits*	97	85	-12
Paid time off – Holidays	99	81	-17
Paid time off – Vacations	99	79	-20

Source: Bureau of Labor Statistics. Employment Benefits in Medium and Large Firms, June 1985, Bulletin 2237; Bureau of Labor Statistics. Economic Benefits in the United States – March 2014, USDL-14-1348
*Under the Affordable Care Act, firms with 100 or more employees were required to offer health care benefits to their employees in 2015, as will firms with 50 or more employees in 2016.

Between 1984 and 2014, and in the absence of strong collective bargaining or regulatory mandates, work benefits including paid time off, retirement, and healthcare declined. As shown in Table 1, in the mid-1980s, these benefits were offered by nearly all of the large (100 or more employees) firms in the United States; by the mid-2010s, access to healthcare and paid time off had declined to approximately 85 percent and 80 percent of the employees of large firms respectively. Retirement benefits are now offered by slightly more firms than they were 30 years ago, but the nature of retirement benefits has changed significantly. In the early-1980s, more workers were covered by defined benefits plans (pensions) than by defined contribution plans (401k plans), a balance that has since reversed. The boost that had been given to work benefits by the wage and price controls regulations of the World War II years has started to erode.

One additional characteristic of the American labor market concerns income distribution. The most frequently used measure of income inequality in a country is the Gini index - which measures the extent to which the distribution of income among individuals or households within an economy deviates from a perfectly equal distribution. Among OECD countries, earning inequality for full-time employees is highest in Chile, the U.S. and Portugal, while Switzerland, Belgium and Denmark are the countries with the most equality in compensation among their full time employees[27]. Those in the lowest quartile of earnings in the U.S. are the least likely to have access to work benefits of any kind.

Education – a Faltering U.S. Competitive Advantage

For most Americans, education is and has been the key to upward mobility. In 1979, a person with a college degree earned approximately 37 percent more than a person with a high school degree, a number which rose to 76 percent by 2011[28]. A number of factors may have contributed to this. The decline of union representation and collective bargaining as well as an erosion of the inflation-adjusted value of the minimum wage during the 1980s served to increase the disparity between the income levels of the two segments. Further, advances in technology during the 1990s enabled companies to reduce clerical and production labor while increasing their staffing of people with advanced technical training and strong problem-solving skills[29]. While college graduates with non-technical degrees still earn much more than high school graduates, the premium has begun to decline, falling from 86 percent in 2005 to 75 percent in 2012[30].

Compared with other industrialized countries, the U.S. no longer has a distinct competitive advantage in the educational attainment of its workforce. While the tertiary educational attainment rate in the U.S. among those aged 55 to 64 is 73 percent higher than the average for countries that are members of the OECD, the comparable advantage for those aged 25 to 34 is 12 percent[31]. While 40 percent of adults in the U.S. aged 25 to 34 have earned a tertiary degree, the comparative number for Canada as well as for Korea is 56 percent; the number for Japan is 54 percent[32].

Perhaps more telling is that the mean literacy scores of adults (aged 25 – 64) in the U.S. is below the average for OECD countries for those who have not completed secondary education (10.5 percent below average) as well as for those who have completed it (3.7 percent below average). Among adults in the U.S. who have completed tertiary education, the literacy rate is at the OECD average (100.2 percent of average)[33]. The educational advantage held by the U.S. over other countries was owned by a generation that is now approaching retirement; the next generations are nearing parity with the other nation members of the OECD.

Working Hours

Employees in the U.S., on average, work more hours than do employees in other countries. One argument for this is that taxation systems work to shape cultural values and the marginal tax rates on labor are smaller in the U.S. than in most European countries[34]. Another argument is that Europeans have more access to collective bargaining than do Americans[35], something that works to limit hours of work while increasing wages and benefits. Also compelling is the assessment that Americans are more confident than Europeans that hard work is the key to advancement and so are more ready to embrace longer work hours[36,37], a difference in perception that can be traced back to the colonial and early industrial eras in the United States[38]. There is also a culturally-based argument that Europeans simply value time off more than their American counterparts[39]. The issue is far from settled and it may be that some or all of these arguments - separately or in combination - may be helping to influence the amount of time that Americans dedicate to work, but the result is that Americans do spend more time at work than do Europeans.

Demographic Developments

The years between 1970 and 2012 also saw some dramatic changes in American households. The number of households that were "family households", that is, that had at least two members related by birth, marriage, or adoption, declined from 81 percent in 1970 to 66 percent in 2012. During the same time, the share of households that were composed of married couples with children who were under 18 years of age decreased from 40 to 20 percent. The decrease in married couples with children was partially offset by an increase from 17 percent to 27 percent in the proportion of one-person households[40].

Further, the demographics of the workforce have changed. The average age of the American workforce is increasing not just because the baby boom generation (people born between 1946 and 1964) have gotten older, but also because a larger portion of people aged 65 and over continue to work. (See chapter 3.) Also, the workforce has, over the last five decades, become more gender balanced. (See chapter 2.) Heading into the decades from 2020 to 2050, perhaps the most significant impacts on the American workforce will be seen from two intertwining trends: a downward trend in labor force participation rates and a slow growth of the total population.

The decrease in labor force participation rate is expected to be widespread and is forecast to be found among men, women, teenagers and young adults, the 25 to 54 year age group, and baby boomers[41]. Also, over the next several decades, the growth rate of the population of the U.S. is expected to slow due to factors including the aging of baby boomers, declining fertility rates and a decrease in net immigration. The growth rate of the population peaked during the 1970s at approximately 2.6 percent, a number that fell to 1.6 percent during the 1980s, 1.3 percent during the 1990s, and declined to 0.7 percent during the 2000s -- a level that is expected to remain for the next several decades[42].

Changes in the structure of American families may affect the degree to which child and elder care is needed by people engaged in the workforce, and consequently, in the types of benefits organizations may have to offer in order to attract and retain qualified employees during periods of low unemployment. Similarly, changes in the age of the workforce, the participation rate of individuals in work and the growth of the population each can be expected to have an impact on the overall structure of compensation and work benefits. A low population growth and a declining labor force participation rate will contribute to a modest economic growth rate, an environment in which there likely be little impetus to offer more robust compensation and benefit packages to attract employees.

Summary

The first government-endorsed work benefits can be traced to Germany in the late 19ᵗʰ century, a product of societal development that tended toward Socialism. Otto von Bismarck, the first Chancellor of Germany and a central figure in its history, instituted a series of social protections to placate the rising Socialist movement and avoid civil unrest. At his inspiration, Germany adopted early forms of social security that addressed health care and retirement benefits.

The concept was slow to migrate to the United States. In the middle of the 19ᵗʰ century - the beginning of the American industrial revolution - work benefits were scarce both because industrialists had little interest in offering them and because workers were primarily focused on pay and working conditions. At the onset of the 20ᵗʰ century, the movement toward Socialism that had been growing in Eastern Europe gained a toehold in the United States. The Russian Revolution of 1905-6[43], along with ones in Poland[44], and other Eastern European nations were a forceful reminder of the strength of the social change that was occurring overseas. A small but vocal Socialist Party in the U.S. led by Eugene Debs, a former union organizer, earned six percent of the popular vote in presidential elections in 1912 and three percent in 1920.

The "industrial demands" of the American Socialist Party remained largely unaddressed until the Great Depression. Franklin Delano Roosevelt's "New Deal" legislation established minimum wages and the monitoring of working conditions, encouraged the formation of unions, established social security, unemployment insurance, aid to blind, deaf and disabled workers, prohibited child labor and set a limit on the length of the workweek. These were significant steps toward establishing enforceable social protections for workers and their families.

The era of World War II saw advances as well as retrenchments in worker protections. Fearful of inflation during the war years, Congress passed legislation that established wage and price controls, but exempted work benefits from these limits. Organizations began using enhanced work benefits as a recruiting tool and benefit packages including healthcare and retirement options were soon offered to a majority of American full time workers. After the war, unions adopted work benefits as one of their principal causes.

Beginning in the 1970s and in the decades that followed, Congressional sponsorship of worker protection legislation has declined. Two exceptions to this general rule were the passage of the Family and Medical Leave Act of 1993 and the Affordable Care Act of 2010. At the same time, union membership as a percentage of the total American workforce declined significantly since its heyday in the 1950s. Without strong Congressional or union advocacy, work benefits returned to their earlier status as something to be negotiated for by individuals in their employment contracts. Consequently, worker access to benefits including healthcare and paid time off declined between the 1980s and the 2010s and retirement benefits migrated from defined benefit to defined contribution systems. (See chapter 3). The decline in access to work benefits has been most strongly felt by those in the lowest quartile of earnings. (See chapter 2).

Changes in the American workforce may also have helped to shape benefit offerings. During the last five decades, Americans have become increasingly well-educated, but not as quickly as in many other nations. Further, literacy rates among Americans with less than a college education have fallen behind those of other industrialized nations. The United States, whose workforce once held an educational attainment advantage over other nations, is in danger of falling behind them.

On the other hand, the U.S. workforce spends more time at work than do its counterparts in other countries, partly for cultural reasons, partly because of disparities in the marginal income tax rates in most European countries versus those in the U.S., and partly because collective bargaining is more prevalent in Europe than it is in the U.S. This work motivation may also be fueled by differences in income distribution within the U.S. versus those in most other industrialized nations. The relatively high disparity between the higher and lower income strata in the U.S. makes a transition from "starter" to "career" jobs a necessary step if a person wishes to lead a middle-class (or higher) lifestyle. For this to be sustainable, however, requires a balanced long-term growth in lower-, middle-, and upper-income jobs.

Changes in family structure, the age and other demographic characteristics of the American workforce may equally have contributed to the nature of benefits that are being offered. Going forward, lower population growth and a surge in elder care may become workplace concerns and affect the way in which people prepare for retirement. Declines in the need for family-friendly benefits for childcare may be offset by increases in the need for eldercare. Further, over the next several decades, the population is expected to grow only slowly and workforce participation is expected to decline, factors that tend to indicate that the long term forecast for work benefits for the average worker is that they may be expected to continue their slow and steady decline.

2 ENVIRONMENTAL INFLUENCES ON BENEFIT OFFERINGS

"'In the tropics one must before everything keep calm.'
... He lifted a warning forefinger... 'Du calme, du calme. Adieu.'"

Joseph Conrad
Heart of Darkness (1899)

Background

Perhaps the most frequently cited argument for why organizations adopt certain types of work benefits is that they want to match or better their competitors in their total compensation packages. Firms do tend to imitate each other, to develop similar organizational structures and so to hire similarly qualified people[1]. Offering a package of work benefits to which people are attracted has been shown to increase employee commitment to a firm, to heighten employee job satisfaction and to lower turnover rates[2]. But as the brief histories for each of the categories of benefits in chapters three through seven will show, there are environmental factors that cause certain types of benefits to become popular. This chapter will show how changes in the gender balance of the workforce, in government regulation, and in the economy have affected benefit offerings.

The Changing Workforce

The last half-century has witnessed a dramatic shift in the composition of the American workforce, and one of the largest changes has been its gender makeup. In 1960, the workforce of the U.S. was 33 percent female; as of 2013, that number had grown to 47 percent[3]. Several factors contributed to this:

The post-World War II era saw a domestic division of labor defined by "breadwinner versus caregiver" roles for males and females. This was held to be a cultural ideal even though during World War II U.S. factories had hired women and had created federally-funded child care centers[4]. The post-war years were a time when female domesticity was considered the norm, but it was also a time when a quest for a higher standard of living coupled with rising prices provided an impetus for mothers to return to the workforce, even if only on a part-time basis and after children in the household had entered school[5]. Also, in the post-World War II era and through the Vietnam War, the G.I. Bill - with its education and housing benefits - was one that worked largely to the benefit of males and helped to create and reinforce the expectation that men would be better educated and trained and more aptly suited to the workplace than women[6].

A Cultural Shift

For females to re-enter the job market in large numbers required several things: (1) a cultural shift away from the expectation that women would be confined to "caregiving" roles and be the sole "caregivers" within a family to a sharing of that role with men, (2) an increase in the level of female educational attainment, and (3) some accommodation by hiring organizations to enable parents of both genders to fulfill their "caregiving" roles.

The gradual return of females to the workforce depended on a confluence of political and social changes that redefined the role of women in American society. As the workforce began its trend toward a balance between the genders, an increasing number of organizations began to be staffed with employees who had non-work priorities such as the caretaking for children and/or elderly household members.

In the 1960's, the division of household tasks among those engaged in a dual-income marital relationship was largely unaffected by the female's employment[7]. Women took on outside-the-home employment as an addition to their domestic duties. A decade later, married working women with children spent less time on household chores than their non-working counterparts, but male members of these households contributed the same number of hours to household tasks whether or not their spouses were employed[8]. More recent studies have shown a gradual shift toward a balanced approach to the sharing of household tasks. When females are employed in middle class (as opposed to working class) professions and members of dual-parent households, the division of household tasks shifts from being primarily the responsibility of females to being the shared responsibility of both parents[9].

The division of labor within the household contributes to an understanding of the impact of the rise of dual income households because the time needed to upkeep of a household, to maintain a social life, to care for family, etc., can contribute to stress. "Work–life conflict" is a concept that gained notoriety in the 1980s when the female labor force participation rate had begun to exceed 50 percent[10]. It assumes that there is a limited amount of time for a person to allocate to work (career and career development) and to non-work or lifestyle pursuits (health, pleasure, leisure, family and spiritual development) and that these alternate uses of time compete for attention[11]. The rise in dual income households coupled with an increase in the sharing of caregiving responsibilities translates to a need for flexible work options by members of both genders. And as much as these are in demand by dual income households, they are needed even more so by single parent ones.

As part of a social movement, the quest for equality in the workplace (as well as in other social contexts) had very direct and personal consequences in the lives of its supporters[12]. One of the guiding principles of this movement was social justice, defined in terms of equal access to employment. Another impetus for this was simple consumerism; people in search of a more comfortable life were willing to seek work outside the home to achieve it[13]. While the argument social justice demands equal opportunity in the workplace is compelling, so too is the argument that the superior economic status of the dual income household was something that families desired. While these two lines of reasoning do not overlap, neither are they mutually exclusive.

Educational Attainment

Second, the educational attainment of females, well below that of males in the 1960s, rose gradually over the last few decades and now exceeds that of males. In 1970, 13.5 percent of adult males and 8.1 percent of adult females had completed a bachelor's degree or higher; by 2014 the balance in these numbers had reversed – 32.0 percent of females and 31.9 percent of males had achieved this level of education. As shown in Table 2, as of 2014, a larger percentage of the female population of the U.S. had completed an associate's, bachelors' or master's degree than had their male counterparts. Further, between 1970 and 2009 among those people who had completed high school and were between 16 and 24 years old, the college enrollment of males increased from 55 to 66 percent; for females it increased from 49 to 74 percent[14].

Table 2

Educational Attainment of the Population
25 Years and Over
Percent of Population
2014

	Male	Female	Total
Up to 11th grade	12.3	11.1	11.7
High School Graduate	30.5	29.0	29.7
Some College, no degree	16.4	17.0	16.7
Associate's Degree	8.9	10.9	9.9
Bachelor's Degree	20.0	20.4	20.2
Master's Degree	7.8	9.1	8.5
Professional Degree	1.8	1.2	1.5
Doctoral Degree	2.3	1.3	1.8

Source: U.S. Census: Educational Attainment in the United States – 2014, Table 2

In 2013, women accounted for 51 percent of all workers employed in management, professional, and related occupations, slightly more than their share of total employment (47 percent)[15]. Further, for those in professional and technical trades, highly educated mothers displayed a greater labor market attachment than less educated mothers[16]. Women have become a committed, educated and integrated part of professional America.

In order to hire a female workforce, organizations had to provide benefits that would ease work-family conflict. That employees have non-work priorities necessitates either that the number of hours that employees work are predictable, that their hours are flexible, or that absolute amount of time they spent on their jobs is limited[17]. Flextime and teleworking, job characteristics that apply most frequently to management, professional and related professions, were adopted by organizations largely in response to a need to accommodate the dual breadwinner/caregiver roles that their employees, both male and female, were undertaking.

Legislative Factors

The federal legislature facilitated the growth of benefits in two ways: One, it worked to ensure that females would have equal pay and working conditions with males, thereby supporting the growth in female labor force participation from the 1970s through the present. Two, it established (under certain conditions) a requirement that private sector firms place-hold jobs for parents who take leave for the birth or adoption of a child. And three, it made health care a mandatory work benefit for medium and larger sized firms.

Several acts passed by Congress and signed into law have addressed gender discrimination in the workplace (i.e., the Equal Pay Act of 1963, Title VII of the Civil Rights Act of 1964, the Pregnancy Discrimination Act of 1978). [Note: The Pregnancy Discrimination Act ensured that pregnant women would be treated no differently than males in the workplace[18], but it did not establish pregnant females as a protected class of individuals or entitle them to any special rights or privileges. The nature of the protection that it ensured was to prevent discriminatory treatment of pregnant females rather than to provide special safety measures for them.] These laws did not directly promote the creation of benefits within private sector firms in the U.S., but they were designed to ensure that females would have the same pay and working conditions as males in the workforce.

The Act that most directly addressed family and work is the Family and Medical Leave Act of 1993 (FMLA). The FMLA was passed in order to give assurance to workers that their jobs would not be at risk in the event that they needed time away from work to care for a new child or an ill parent, spouse or child[19] or for the employee's own serious health condition[20]. While the FMLA addressed the conditions surrounding the birth or adoption of an infant or a medical emergency of an immediate family member, it was not intended to provide a long term solution to the conflicts inherent in parenting and work. The FMLA established a "floor" rather than a ceiling for employees' rights; its effect was to turn the practice of unpaid parental leave from a point in an employer-employee negotiation to a nationwide mandate for larger employers. Since the law has no expiration date, its passage marked the establishment of a labor right[21].

While the increase in female participation in the labor force was the precipitating cause of the establishment of a family leave right under the FMLA, its importance and impact was left largely unrecognized in the discussions leading to the passage of the bill at the national level. Congress passed the FMLA on the stated premise that it would enhance organizational productivity. Arguments promoting work-life balance or establishing or enhancing any other labor rights have generally not been cited in the preambles of employment regulations; justifications for employment regulations have generally been phrased in terms of advancing business interests[22].

Complementary legislation introduced to Congress between 1993 and 2011 on the topic of work-life balance or expanding the reach of the FMLA has not met with success. A number of bills have been introduced into the U.S. House and Senate to promote work-life balance, establish an insurance fund to provide compensation to people who have taken leave under the FMLA, and to make the benefits of the FMLA available to those who work for companies employing 25 – as opposed to 50 – people or more, but none of these has emerged from the committees to which they were assigned.

The Patient Protection and Affordable Care Act of 2010 extends health care coverage to individuals in part by requiring medium to large sized firms to offer it as a work benefit. The arguments for and against the passage of the Affordable Care Act were many, but among them was one that stemmed from the passage of the Emergency Medical Treatment and Active Labor Act of 1986. This law requires any hospital participating in Medicare to provide emergency care to anyone who needs immediate treatment whether or not the recipient of the treatment has the ability to pay for it. By doing this, the cost of treatment for non-paying recipients of care is borne by hospitals providing the care, which, to remain solvent, have to reallocate those costs to those patients who personally or through insurance coverage can afford to pay for their services. With the percent of the civilian labor force receiving health care benefits declining from 97 percent to 85 percent between 1984 and 2014 and trending downward, this redistribution of costs was poised to grow. The Affordable Care Act mandate to provide a health care benefit lessens this redistribution effect while, at the same time, establishes a labor protection.

Economic Factors

Following the end of World War II, the U.S. entered a period of economic expansion. From the 1950s through the 1970s, manufacturing businesses continued to grow at a slow pace, but service businesses began to grow rapidly and the economy shifted from one driven by manufacturing to one driven by services. This created a small demand for labor in the manufacturing sector and a much larger one in the newly burgeoning service sector. The influx of females into the job market helped not only to quench the demand for labor, but to increase the demand for goods and services. The rise of dual income households also fueled an increase in discretionary spending.

The growth of service businesses - organizations in which employees assist customers rather than produce physical goods for sale - had two conflicting effects on the rate at which organizations offer benefits:

Service firms are more likely to adopt family-friendly work benefits than are manufacturing firms[23], and firms staffed by professionals are especially likely to do so[24]. In short, the U.S. economy's long term trend toward service businesses and away from goods producing sectors had a positive impact on the degree to which organizations were willing to offer family-friendly work benefits.

On the other hand, the substantial growth in service economy jobs tended to be at the lower end of the wage scale, where benefits, in line with pay, tend to be less robust[25]. The growth in lower end service jobs has been so pronounced that these jobs, which were at one time the entry level positions people took to begin their careers, have become career positions themselves. Also, service-based organizations tend to have smaller (and, therefore, less regulated) average firms sizes than manufacturing organizations[26]. The Family and Medical Leave Act, for example, applies only to those firms with fifty or more full time equivalent employees[27]. Further, larger firms tend to offer more benefits than do the smaller firms because institutional pressures to imitate competitors are more strongly felt by larger firms than by smaller ones[28]. Larger firms also tend to "set the standard for other employers with systems of internal labor markets, job security, health insurance, and retirement benefits, and thus have a substantial influence on the nature of the employment market in the United States[29]."

Over the three decades leading to 2015, the trend in access to benefits in the U.S. was a negative one. Access to healthcare and paid time off decreased significantly among workers in firms that employ 100 or more workers, a decline that was even more pronounced among smaller firms. Retirement benefits increased, but a part of the increase can be attributed to the switch from defined benefit to defined contribution programs as discussed in chapter 3. Even with this change, only about two thirds of private industry employees in the U.S. have access to some form of retirement benefit. Going forward, this trend may in part be expected to reverse under provisions of the Patient Protection and Affordable Care Act of 2010 that require medium and larger firms to offer healthcare benefits to their employees (See chapter 5).

The Recession of 2008 - 2011

Benefits are an integrated part of a total compensation package and are responsive to the forces of supply and demand in the labor markets. The relatively high level of unemployment experienced in the U.S. between 2008 and 2011 may have contributed to the decline in the rate at which benefits were offered by private sector firms during that time.

Between 2008 and 2011, when unemployment rates were at their highest since the early 1980's[30], employers may have felt less pressure to offer superior salaries and/or benefits in order to meet their labor needs. In competitive markets, availability and participation in "perks" or benefits is dependent on the same factors that determine income[31]. During better economic times, characterized by lower levels of unemployment, organizations focus on employee retention practices such as training, reward and employee involvement systems. During more lean economic times and ones which are marked by high levels of unemployment, these practices receive less support[32].

Partly because service businesses tend to offer fewer benefits than goods producing firms and the substantial growth in employment in the U.S. over the last three decades has been concentrated in service establishments, the overall rate at which benefits are being offered has decreased. Two shifts in benefit patterns emerged immediately before and at the beginning of the recession of 2008 – 2011. The first concerned the rate at which small firms (fewer than 100 employees) granted benefits to their employees. As can be seen in Graph 1, paid holiday and vacation time were offered by 84 percent and 88 percent of small firms, respectively, in 1990; by 2010, both paid holidays and vacation time were each offered by 70 percent of small firms. The decline in healthcare benefits was gradual, peaking in 1992 at 71 percent and then stabilizing at 42 percent beginning in 2003. Retirement benefits declined only modestly, from 42 percent to 35 percent between 1990 and 2010.

Graph 1

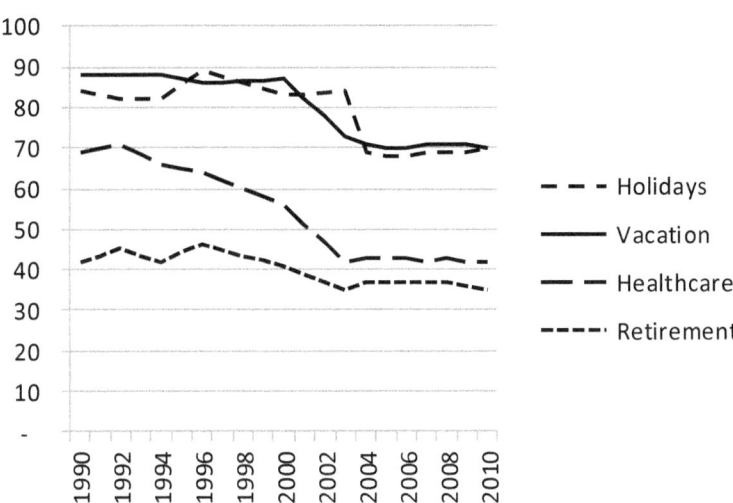

Benefits Offered in Small Firms
Percent of Small Firms with Paid Holidays,
Vacation, Healthcare and Retirement Benefits
1990 - 2010
Percent

Source: Employee Benefits Research Institute; Databook on Employee Benefits, Chapter 4: Participation in Employee Benefit Programs, March 2011.

The decline in benefits in the years leading up to the recession may simply have been a coincidence, or it may have been leading indicator of troubled times to come. When the recession did take hold in 2008, little happened to the rate at which small firms offered paid time off, healthcare and retirement benefits. Once the benefit offering rate had reached its new lower mark (70 percent for paid time off, 40 percent for healthcare and retirement), it seems to have stabilized.

The second of the trends that appeared during the 2008 – 2011 recession was the degree to which firms hired workers on a part-time rather than a full-time basis. As shown in Graph 2, the number of workers who took part time jobs either because work was slower than normal (slack work) or because part time jobs were the only ones available spiked at the onset of the recession. Not only was the upturn in part time work coincident with the beginning of the recession, the reasons given by survey respondents for taking work on a part-time, as opposed to full time basis, were directly related to the economic downturn.

Graph 2

Part Time Employment Level – Seasonally Adjusted
People Taking Part-Time Work for Economic Reasons
All Industries, 2005 – 2015, in Thousands

Part-time
Workers

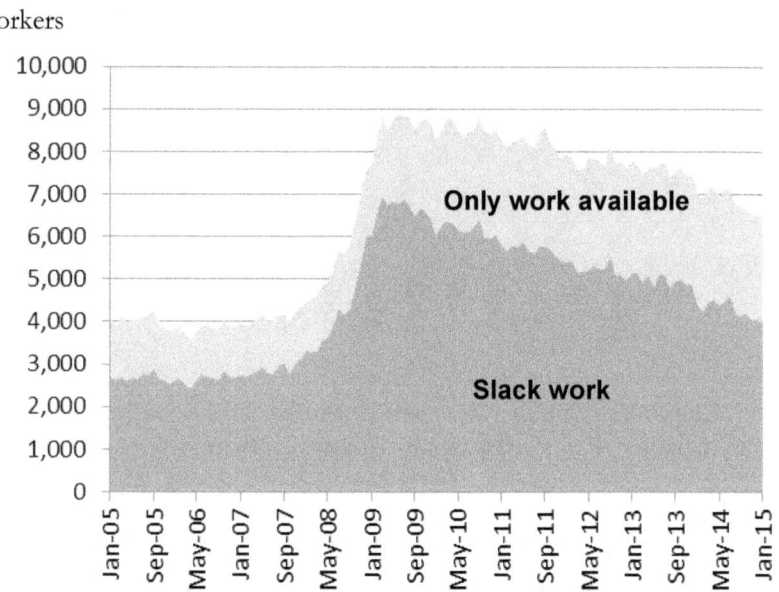

Source: Bureau of Labor Statistics, Labor Force Statistics from the Current Population Survey, Series IDs: LNS12032195 and LNS12032196

Between 2005 and 2007, an average of approximately 3.9 million workers took part time jobs for reasons stemming from a slow business environment; by June of 2009, the number had risen to 8.8 million and has been declining slowly and steadily since that time. The rise in part time labor had the effect of lowering the rate at which benefits were available to workers. As highlighted in Table 3, the disparity between access to health, retirement and paid time off benefits between full and part time workers is significant.

Table 3

Access to Selected Benefits
Part Time Versus Full Time Employees
U.S. Civilian Workforce - 2014
Percent of Employees with Access to Selected Benefits

	Private Industry		State & Local Government	
	Full Time	Part Time	Full Time	Part Time
Paid Sick Leave	74	24	98	41
Paid Vacation	91	35	66	21
Paid Holidays	90	37	74	30
Health Care	86	23	99	24
Retirement	74	37	99	38

Sources: Bureau of Labor Statistics, Economic News Release, July 25, 2014 Tables 1, 2, and 6

When the recession of 2008 struck, the upturn in the number of part-time (as opposed to full-time) workers was correlated with a decrease in the number of American workers who had access to work benefits, a significant cost savings for the corporations who altered the full- versus part-time status of their employees. One of the effects of having work benefits be part of the compensation negotiation between management and labor is that the availability of paid leave or retirement benefits to workers can be diminished or withdrawn at the discretion of management.

Summary

From the perspective of a human resources department, a view of the job market, an understanding of what a firm can afford to offer, and a survey of the benefits offered by competitors helps greatly to shape the benefits package that a firm will likely offer. In addition to these considerations, several environmental factors may also contribute to the rate at which benefits are being offered.

First, an understanding of trends in the demographics of the workforce can give a forward-thinking firm an ability to recruit people, especially those that have not traditionally been part of the firm's labor market. In a macro sense, this was the case with a long term trend toward gender balance in the workplace. A cultural change following World War II made it not only acceptable, but a mark of social justice that women should have equal access to employment. Educational attainment between the genders slowly balanced and women entered the workforce in large numbers. For people already in the workforce, female educational attainment now exceeds that of males and current college enrollments suggest that disparity will continue to grow. With women interested in working and attaining the educational credentials to do so, organizations began to adopt family friendly work benefits.

Second, laws passed over the last several decades also contributed to a gender balanced workplace. The Equal Pay Act of 1963, Title VII of the Civil Rights Act of 1964, the Pregnancy Discrimination Act of 1978, the Family and Medical Leave Act of 1993 and the Patient Protection and Affordable Care Act of 2010 are among the most important of these. These largely worked to ensure that women would have equal access to employment and equal pay with males for the work they do (something yet to be fully realized). Also, an accommodation for working parents was the Family and Medical Leave Act, which required medium and large sized businesses to allow parents to take up to twelve weeks of unpaid leave on the birth or adoption of a child or for other family medical emergencies.

Third, economic factors, both long and short term, affect benefit offering rates. In the longer term, the growth in employment in business in the U.S. over the last five decades has largely been in smaller service firms. Smaller firms are less likely to offer benefits than are larger firms, and service firms less likely to offer benefits than manufacturing firms. Both of these factors have contributed to the decrease in the availability of benefits to private sector employees over the last three decades. The economy is poised to continue this trend.

Short term economic trends also affect benefit offering rates. The level of compensation – wages as well as work benefits - that is offered to new employees is very much subject to labor market conditions, and benefit packages can be renegotiated with existing employees at any time. The changeover from defined benefit to defined contribution retirement plans is evidence of this, as are recent changes in health plans. The newer retirement and health plans give firms more flexibility in adjusting their contribution levels at any point.

Work benefits offerings also reflect societal changes. Family friendly work benefits became popular when the workplace was becoming gender neutral. When women entered the workforce in large numbers, the increase in the available labor pool had a dampening effect on total compensation levels, making it worthwhile for firms to consider flexible work options and other family friendly accommodations. This was in part because women have historically earned less than men working in comparable positions. While this was a socially beneficial event and one that enabled the U.S. to remain globally competitive, within the simple short term relationship of supply and demand, and increase in the supply of a resource causes its price to decrease. The added labor supply had a depressing effect on overall compensation and benefits, but the consequent emergence of dual income and single parent households increased the demand for flexible work options like flextime and telework.

The trend toward decreased benefit offerings is poised to continue. The social, political and economic factors that aligned to promote the creation of flexible work characteristics simultaneously worked to take away the impetus for firms to offer retirement, paid time off and health care benefits. Firms interested in managing budgets and mitigating risks effected structural cost-saving changes in retirement and health care plans and simply began offering paid time off less often than they had decades ago.

3 RETIREMENT

"That is no country for old men."

William Butler Yeats
Sailing to Byzantium (1928)

Background

The term "retirement" means a complete and permanent withdrawal from paid labor[1]. During the colonial and early industrial ages in the United States, people simply did not retire; they worked as long as they were able, taking less physically taxing jobs as they aged and relying more on the help of others. A Puritan ethic attributed a moral preeminence to work, holding usefulness as a mark within society. In the colonial era, work was a defense against the permanent threat of scarcity and production was a measure of economic health[2].

The first retirement benefits to be offered in the U.S. date back to the Colonial era. For more than a century before the Revolutionary War began, the British colonies gave pensions to disabled soldiers and sailors. On August 26, 1776, the first pension legislation of the new U.S. was passed. The Continental Congress provided half pay for soldiers and sailors - officers as well as enlisted men – who were disabled in the military service and who were incapable of earning a living. The pay continued as long as the person was disabled. During and after the Revolutionary War, the Federal government expanded upon this and created three types of pensions for people in the military service and their dependents: disability pensions for servicemen who were injured in the line of duty; service pensions to those who served for a set minimum amount of time; and widows' pensions for those women whose husbands had qualified for a service pension or had been killed in the line of duty[3]. Private pensions and retirement plans would not arrive for another century.

Industrialization

Pre-industrial America's economy was largely composed of family-owned businesses; there were farms and shops, small manufacturing firms, and international import and export companies[4]. Firms - the size that Sears, Roebuck and Company would be in 1916 with its thousands of employees – would have been inconceivable to the generations living up to and including the 1840s[5]. Spurred by the growth of the textile and railroad industries, states began to feel pressure to create the legal framework for a form of business that would allow for the collection of large amounts of capital, the employment of large numbers of workers, and management by people other than a firm's principal owners. In 1811, New York was the first state to enact a general incorporation statute for manufacturing companies; in the 1830s New York was followed by Pennsylvania, Connecticut, Maryland, and Michigan in enacting legislation to this effect[6].

Industrialization was beginning to change the landscape of employment in America. The population was growing quickly and moving to urban centers. By mid-century, Thoreau characterized the U.S. as a "place of business" with "infinite bustle.[7]" As the industrial revolution began to release people from the specter of scarcity, their thoughts shifted from work and productivity to consumption and leisure[8].

The growth of larger businesses did several things to the workplace: It enabled businesses to hire more specialized labor that could focus on specific categories of tasks and to reap the benefits of the efficiencies that attended to it. It allowed for training and development, for career paths, and perhaps most importantly, for salaries and wages that were far superior to those that could be earned working on the family farm.

The late nineteenth and early twentieth centuries saw the confluence of several separate events that worked to popularize the concept that retirement was an acceptable if not desirable state of affairs for the elderly. First, industrialization was helping to spur the growth of a middle class in the U.S. – people who were not affluent, but who could afford to save some portion of their earnings. Second, military pensions were far more commonly available than at any time in the history of the U.S. prior to this time.

Graph 3

Labor Force Participation Rates
Men Aged 65 and Over
U.S. 1850 to 2016 (forecast)

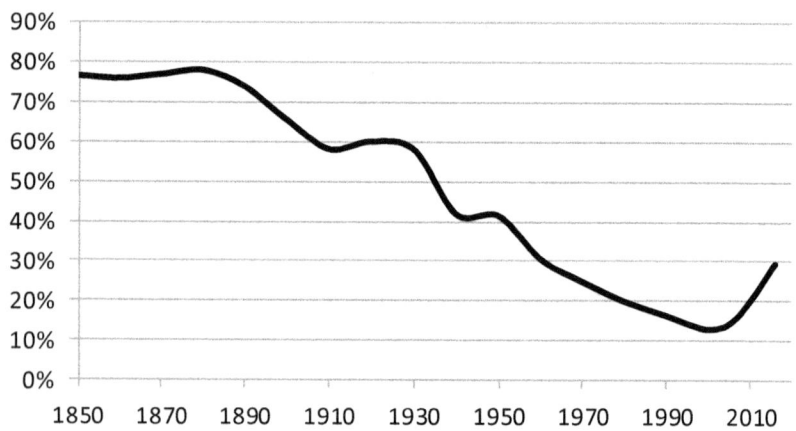

Sources: Costa, D. (1998). *The evolution of retirement: An American economic history, 1880-1990.* Chicago: The University of Chicago Press; Bureau of Labor Statistics, U.S. Department of Labor, *The Economics Daily,* Projected growth in labor force participation of seniors, 2006-2016.

By 1900, approximately 21 percent of all white males in the U.S. who were aged 55 and over were receiving pension payments from the federal government based on their having served in the Union army during the Civil War[9]. As shown in Graph 3, labor force participation rates among men aged 65 and over had begun to fall at the turn of the century; approximately half of the decline in labor force participation among this segment occurred before Social Security legislation was enacted in 1935. Also noteworthy is that the rate of retirement of elder males is projected to rise through the early part of the twenty-first century.

Private Retirement Plans

The first organization in the U.S. to establish a private pension plan was the American Express Company in 1875. In order to qualify for a retirement benefit, an employee had to have 20 years of service, be aged 60 years or more, and be disabled. The company's general manager would have to recommend a person for retirement subject to the approval of the executive committee of the board of directors[10]. Within a few years, other companies began initiating retirement programs. In 1880, the Baltimore and Ohio Railroad established a retirement plan financed by both the employer and the employees[11], and was intended to cover all of its workers as they attained the age of 65. At the time, few people lived to be this age. In 1900, the average life expectancy for males in the U.S. was 46.3, and 48.3 for females; it was not until 1949 that the average life expectancy for males passed the 65 year mark[12].

Retirement benefits have long been the subject of federal as well as state legislation. The Revenue Act of 1928 exempted income from pension trusts from current taxation[13]. The income from these trusts was tax-deferred; it was taxed when it was withdrawn, presumably after the beneficiary of the trust retired. Ten years later, the Revenue Act of 1938 made pension trusts irrevocable and established a rule that funds could not be diverted from them[14]. In 1942, the Act was further amended to limit allowable deductions, integrate the disbursements with Social Security payments, and to prohibit the payments from being stratified as to officers and non-officers of the organization[15].

The Labor-Management Relations Act of 1947 established the National Labor Relations Board to oversee disputes between organized labor and management; it outlawed closed shops (agreements between a union and management that union membership is a condition of employment), and permitted unions to represent the workers of an organization on a majority vote of its employees. Under the law, a union would only be able to use the facilities of the National Labor Relations Board if it had filed financial reports along with an affidavit that its union officers were not communists[16], a provision nullified in 1965 by the Supreme Court[17]. It was sponsored in Congress in 1947 by Senator Robert Taft and Representative Fred Hartley, and became known as the Taft-Hartley Labor Act. It was vetoed by President Truman[18] but the law was passed by Congress over his veto. The Act provided guidelines for the creation and management of pension trusts to be administered jointly by employers and unions[19]. The following year, the National Labor Relations Board determined that pensions were a part of employee compensation, and so were subject to the bargaining agreements over which it had jurisdiction[20].

The Welfare and Pension Plan Disclosure Act of 1962 shifted the responsibility for the protection of pension fund assets from individual sponsors to the Pension and Benefits Welfare Administration[21], a program of the federal government. While this act would eventually be repealed and replaced by the Employment Retirement Income Security Act (ERISA) of 1974[22], the oversight of pension assets would remain with the U.S. Government. The ERISA is administered in part by the Employee Benefits Security Administration (Department of Labor), the Internal Revenue Service, and the Pension Benefit Guaranty Corporation. The Employee Benefits Security Administration is responsible for administering the fiduciary, reporting and disclosure provisions of ERISA, while the Pension Benefits Guarantee Corporation is the agency of the U.S. government that insures private defined benefit pensions against the unfortunate event that a private pension plan cannot meet its obligations to its covered beneficiaries.

The Revenue Act of 1978[23] established qualified deferred compensation plans, commonly referred to as section 401(k) plans, under which employees may elect to defer a certain portion of their compensation until after retirement. The deferred portion of their compensation is taxed only when it is withdrawn. Legislation passed since 1978 has largely worked to refine and manage the types of plans that were established by this Act. In addition, several laws have addressed the development of retirement accounts for people who are self-employed or who own small businesses, government workers and people who work for not-for-profit organizations.

The passage of the Revenue Act of 1978 established the framework for a significant change in the way organizations offer retirement benefits and in the way most workers in the U.S. save for retirement. Prior to the passage of the act, most organizations that offered a retirement benefit offered a "defined benefit" plan, that is, a pension plan in which pension payments were calculated according to length of an employee's service and the salary he or she earned at the time of retirement. After the passage of the Act, most organizations ceased offering defined benefit plans and began offering defined contribution plans - retirement plans in which an employee defers a portion of his or her compensation by setting it aside into a retirement account (a 401k account). To be considered an employee benefit, an employing organization must match some of all of the employee contribution to the account.

The effect of the Revenue Act of 1978 on the way in which employees prepare for retirement was significant. According to the Employee Benefits Research Institute, between 1979 and 2011, the number of private sector participants in defined benefit retirement plans declined from 62 to 7 percent of the workforce. At the same time, the number of participants in defined contribution retirement plans increased from 16 to 69 percent of the workforce[24].

Social Security

The first nationally sponsored retirement program was pioneered in Germany in 1889. Chancellor Otto von Bismarck introduced a pension payable to non-working Germans who were 70 years or older, an age requirement that was reduced to 65 in 1916[25]. The pension was funded by current tax revenues[26], which, given that the average life expectancy of a male born in Prussian circa 1866 was 32.5 years[27], did not portend to be a very expensive national budget item at the time.

In the United States, President Franklin D. Roosevelt established individual retirement benefits when he signed the Social Security Act[28] into law in 1935 as part of the New Deal program. As with the amended German social security system, the age requirement for receiving a disbursement under the law was 65[29]. The life expectancy of a male born in the U.S. in 1935 was 59.9 years; for females it was 63.9 years[30].

The Social Security System was intended to be a job stimulus for younger workers. The stock market had crashed in 1929 and the Great Depression was in its sixth year. At the time, jobs were often held based on seniority, and older workers generally had more job security than did younger ones. Enabling older and generally more expensive workers to retire was a way to open opportunities for younger workers to take their places. The Social Security Act of 1935 contained a provision that if "any qualified individual has received wages with respect to regular employment after he attained the age of sixty-five, the old age benefit payable to such individual shall be reduced, for each calendar month in any part of which such regular employment occurred, by an amount equal to one month's benefit[31]."

After its initial passage, the Social Security Act was amended several times between 1935 and 1972 to increase coverage and benefits for retirees. It was amended in 1939 to add dependent and survivors benefits and again in 1950 to increase the overall benefits levels. A provision for early retirement for women was added in 1956 and a similar provision for men was added in 1961. Automatic cost of living adjustments were instituted in 1972. Beginning in the mid-1970s, however, an increasing life expectancy and a baby-boom in the population caused the Social Security Administration to propose a series of cutbacks and limitations to benefits in the interest of the long term solvency of the program. In 1977 and again in 1983, Federal Insurance Contributions Act (FICA) taxes were raised and benefits were scaled back, and in 1993, the taxable portion of social security benefits was raised from 50 to 85 percent. Recognizing that payments under the Social Security System might not alone be enough to sustain a household, in 2000, the retirement earnings test for those at full retirement age was eliminated[32].

Social Security Systems may be designed as pension plans, that is, flat rate payments to any person who has attained a certain age, for example, sixty-five. They may also be designed as annuities, or payments made to workers (and their families) that are a return on contributions made into the system. Under the first form, everyone who attains a certain age receives the same payment; under the latter form, those who contribute most to the system during their working years receive the most from it in retirement. Most countries have hybrids of the two forms, combining a minimum payment with a sliding scale based on lifelong contributions to the system. Social Security in the U.S. is a hybrid of the two forms, but tends toward the annuity rather than the pension system of payment.

Issues and Trends in Social Security

Social security payments in the U.S. are not designed to provide a pension sufficient for a retiree to live comfortably; these payments are intended to supplement private pensions or savings for the purpose of retirement[33]. As life expectancies continue to increase and the baby boom generation ages and retires, the cost of supporting the Social Security system will rise unless adjustments are made to the program. One such adjustment has been an increase in the full retirement age. Initially set at 65 years, it has been modified for those born between 1938 and 1960; the full retirement age is 65 years for those born in 1938 and gradually increases with each subsequent year. For people born in 1960 or later, the full retirement age is set at 67 years. Other countries with similar social security programs have also increased the age at which full retirement can occur[34]. Other options for adjusting the program include increasing FICA taxes, phasing out the early retirement option, reducing benefits for all recipients or using a means-test to reduce benefits based on the income a retiree receives from other sources.

The Social Security administration offers an early retirement option for those who would prefer to begin their retirement at age 62 rather than 65 or higher. For the average person – a person of average health and life expectancy – income would be maximized by delaying the receipt of social security benefits until full retirement age[35]. However, if a person nearing retirement is ill and has a reduced life expectancy, it may be in his or her best interest to begin retirement early[36].

Several factors contribute to this calculation. As of 2015, people who attained their full retirement age before drawing on their social security benefits will not be taxed on those benefits no matter what income they earn from employment. For a person who retired before attaining his or her full retirement age, for every two dollars he or she earns in excess of a set limit ($15,720 in 2015), one dollar will be withheld from benefits. This is, in effect, a 33 percent marginal income tax on earnings. For a person who retired in the year in which he or she reached full retirement age, for every three dollars he or she earns in excess of a set limit ($41,880 in 2015), one dollar will be withheld from benefits. This is, in effect, a 25 percent marginal income tax on earnings. (Note: This formula has changed frequently over the years; it is best to check with the social security administration for updates.) Under this formula and absent any special reason to expect that a person's life expectancy will be longer or shorter than average, males with low income would benefit by taking an early retirement while males with high income would maximize their benefits by waiting until their full retirement ages. Because females have, on average, a longer life expectancy than males, women of all income levels stand to maximize their benefits by waiting until their full retirement ages[37].

Preparedness for Retirement

In the years immediately following the passage of the Revenue Act of 1978, the retirement plans offered by most organizations switched from defined benefit to defined contribution, more commonly known as 401k plans. There were several beneficial effects of the changeover. First, employees do not have to wait for a vesting period to transpire; contributions made by an employee as well as those made by an employer belong to the employee and travel with the employee if and when he or she changes jobs.

This change places the responsibility for saving for retirement on the employee. Between 2007 and 2010 retirement savings began to decline; it is estimated that 44 percent of U.S. workers in 2010 were not saving adequately for retirement[38]. While education on the topics of health and financial management do help[39], the movement away from defined benefit pensions has had a negative effect on the nation's overall preparedness for retirement.

Table 4

Access to and Participation in Retirement Benefits
U.S. Civilian Workforce - 2014

Percent of Employees with Access to / Participation in Retirement Benefits

Workforce characteristics	Private Industry		State & Local Government	
	Access to	Particip-ation in	Access to	Particip-ation in
Total	65	48	89	91
Occupation				
Management & Financial	80	67	92	83
Professional and Related	84	74	92	83
Services	38	21	84	76
Sales and Related	67	39	n/a	n/a
Office & Administrative	70	56	90	83
Construction & Maintenance	67	53	95	86
Production & Transport	70	53	85	74
Size of Firm				
1 – 49 Workers	45	32	68	60
50 – 99 Workers	63	43	90	81
100 – 499 Workers	78	55	88	80
500 Workers or more	89	77	92	84
Status				
Full time	74	58	99	90
Part time	37	19	38	33
Earnings of full time workers				
Lowest 10 percent	27	11	59	52
Lowest 25 percent	38	18	73	66
Second 25 percent	67	47	93	84
Third 25 percent	76	62	95	86
Highest 25 percent	85	75	98	89
Highest 10 percent	88	79	98	90

Source: Bureau of Labor Statistics, Economic News Release, July 25, 2014 Table 1: Retirement Benefits: Access, Participation, and Take-Up rates.

Further, as shown in Table 4, only 65 percent of employees in private industry have access to retirement benefits through their employers, and only 48 percent of employees participate in these benefits. Those who do participate in retirement benefits tend to have managerial, financial or professional jobs, work full time and for large firms, and tend to be in the upper earnings brackets. Of those who are in the lowest quartile of earnings, only 18 percent are participating in a retirement benefit.

An International Comparative

As of 2011, the U.S. was spending approximately 6.9 percent of its gross domestic product on non-health-related public social programs for the benefit of people aged 65 and over[40]. Like the counterpart programs in most developed nations, the social security system of the U.S. is based on entitlements that develop over time, but it is financed through current tax revenues.

When the social security system was proposed by the Roosevelt administration as part of the New Deal, its purpose was to make jobs available to younger people by taking older people out of the workplace. Until the latter part of the 1990s, it accomplished this by withdrawing benefits payments to anyone who was being paid by an employer. In other countries, social security retirement payments are viewed as a form of social protection – an assurance that a country's elder population will not be living in poverty. The social security system in the U.S. was not designed for this purpose and it has not been effective at accomplishing this mission.

Approximately 24 percent of seniors in the U.S. have incomes below half of the country's median household income – a test for poverty set by the Organisation for Economic Co-operation and Development (OECD). Among OECD countries, only Ireland, Korea and Mexico have higher poverty rates among seniors than does the United States. The high risk of old-age poverty in the U.S. is partly due to the relatively low level of the social security payments, which are set at 18 percent of average earnings – termed a "replacement rate". People who earn relatively little during their lifetimes receive the smallest payments and are at the highest risk of falling below poverty levels. On average, OECD countries provide for social security payments that are 27 percent of a worker's average earnings. Among OECD member nations, only Hungary has a lower replacement rate value (16 percent) for its social security retirement payments than does the U.S.[41]

Summary

The U.S. differs from much of the rest of the world in its approach to the how retirement should be subsidized for people in their elder ages. The United Nations' Declaration of Human Rights envisions "a standard of living adequate for health and well-being" and "security in … old age" as a fundamental human right[42]. The International Labour Organization, a specialized agency of the United Nations, also considers income security a right in old age[43]. Both organizations characterize social security-type payments as part of a social welfare system, a protection for all of a nation's elderly against poverty.

In the United States, social security was designed to be a labor stimulus program for younger workers; it accomplished this by providing a supplemental retirement income to those people (and the families of those people) who participated in the workforce, contributed to the system and who then reached a set minimum age. When it began, it encouraged retirement by providing payments only to those people who withdrew from the workforce. A later amendment to the program allowed for elderly recipients of social security payments to earn pay through work, but taxed them heavily for earnings in excess of a set threshold. Most recently, however, for those people who have attained full retirement age, social security benefits can be received tax-free if they are the only source of a person's income, and, depending on whether the recipient has attained his or her full retirement age, taxed at a reduced rate when combined with income from pensions, wages, interest, dividends and other normally taxable income. In response to these changes, the labor force participation rate of seniors has risen.

Private retirement benefits shifted from defined benefit plans to defined contribution plans after the passage of the Revenue Act of 1978 which established the framework for 401k investment plans. Defined benefit plans were owned and managed by the employer and paid pensions to those workers who met minimum requirements of age and tenure with the firm. Defined contribution plans belong to the employee and do not require a vesting period. There are advantages and disadvantages to each form of retirement benefit, but the distinctive characteristic of the defined contribution plan is that it puts the primary responsibility for retirement planning on the individual rather than on the organization.

Individuals in the U.S. have not all measured up to this task. Slightly less than half of the adult workers in the U.S. (approximately 44 percent) have not and are not saving adequately for retirement. As the compulsion to retire in order to receive social security benefits is no longer part of the social security system structure, elderly workers who are physically capable of working will be able to extend their employment into what would have otherwise been their retirement years. Life expectancies are increasing with advances in medical technology and improved lifestyle choices. Going forward, retirement, as a complete withdrawal from employment, may not be an option available to nearly half of the working population of the U.S.

4 TIME OFF

"Her fear lest the dangerous powers of the subterranean world,
of which she had heard old miners speak,
had been luring him to his destruction…"

E.T.A. Hoffman
The Mines of Falun (1819)

Background

There are many reasons employees want or need to take time off from work. It can be for a vacation, to recover from an illness or to visit a doctor or dentist, for a personal or family reason, because of a disability, and more. Time off is generally categorized according to its purpose[1]:

- Vacation time is intended to provide an extended rest or break from work.

- Sick leave covers those times when an employee is unable to work because of an illness or injury that is not work-related.

- Personal time is a general purpose category and covers those circumstances that do not readily fall into "vacation" or "sick" time

43

categories.

- Family leave (discussed in chapter 6) allows employees time off to care for spouses, children, related elders or other immediate family members, and may be either paid or unpaid leave.

- Disability leave may be short or long term:

    o Short term disability leave entitles a worker to partial or full salary replacement for six to twelve months because of a non-work related illness or injury.

    o Long term disability leave entitles a worker to a partial or full salary replacement after the short term disability leave has been exhausted and can last until the retirement age of the worker.

Leave may also be offered as a combination of vacation, sick and personal time to be allocated among them as may be needed by the employee in any given year. When paid leave is offered but no distinction is made between vacation, sick or personal time, the benefit is usually termed "paid time off" or "consolidated leave".

A Brief History of Vacations

Since the earliest days of Western civilization, rest and leisure has been recognized as a normal custom and practice. The biblical description of creation refers to God as having taken a day of rest after spending six days making and assembling the various aspects of the universe[2]. Aristotle (350 B.C.E.) was one of the earliest advocates of leisure time; he argued that time away from work is what gives people the ability to study the arts and music and to engage generally in intellectual activity[3]. Four hundred years later, some of the first records of vacations began to appear in the Roman Empire. The Bay of Naples provided a holiday destination for the wealthy and leisure class of Rome, and the town of Baiae was perhaps one of Western Civilization's first seaside resorts. Wealthy Romans may even have toured destinations like Turkey and Egypt as part of their cultural education[4].

Vacations have served a number of purposes. Hajj, the Islamic tradition of pilgrimage to Mecca, began in 630 C.E.[5] and as early as the late tenth century, Christian pilgrims were travelling to Rome and Jerusalem[6]. These were expressions of faith as well as a chance to get away from the normal routines of work. Vacations could also be taken as educational experiences. By the sixteenth century, young men from England's elite families began to spend two to four years touring Europe in order to learn the languages, the art and architecture, and the cultures of the Continent. The term "Grand Tour" which became a popular way of describing these extended trips was introduced in a book written in 1670 by Richard Lassels, entitled "Voyage to Italy"[7].

The concept of a vacation was familiar to Colonial era Americans, but it was something that belonged to a wealthy, leisure class[8]. For the remainder of the population, a work ethic strongly influenced by the Puritans equated leisure with idleness and was something fervently to be avoided[9]. Furthermore, to the workers of the Colonial era, living in a free society meant engaging in some form of commerce, agrarian or trade, and earning a profit from one's own business. Family farms and small businesses can be difficult to close and leave behind for vacations.

With the passage of time, however, came a developing industrial economy and a softening of attitudes toward time off. By the late eighteenth century, affluent farmers, merchants and politicians began to take vacations at a series of newly opened resorts that were intended to help people rest and recuperate, offering such services and remedies such as mineral waters, fresh air and exercise[10]. Places like White Sulphur, Saratoga Springs, and Cape May offered a promise of restoring people to good health[11]. The concept gained in popularity and expanded to encompass other forms of recreational activities and amusements. By the 1850s, vacations were a common event among the America's suburban middle class[12]. In the years immediately following the Civil War, people employed in "white collar" occupations customarily received one week's paid vacation, and began to spend this time at summer retreats[13].

In 1910, William Taft, then president of the U.S., along with a number of notable industrialists and bankers, was interviewed by the New York Times for an article on the topic of "How Long Should a Man's Vacation Be?" Taft had been born to a family of lawyers, people who were affluent but not leisure-class, and had spent a significant portion of his adult life in the public service, an occupation that was, at the time, given to generous vacation schedules and government closures during the hot summer months. He responded that "The American people have found out that there is such a thing as exhausting the capital of one's health and constitution and that two or three months' vacation after the hard and nervous strain to which one is subjected during the Autumn and Spring are necessary in order to enable one to continue his work the next year with that energy and effectiveness which it ought to have"[14]. While the statement was made on behalf of the American people, his comments likely represented his own personal experience; it is doubtful that Taft envisioned the whole of the labor force taking extended leave from their work. Nonetheless, Taft's statement and the accompanying statements of the industrialists and bankers contributed to the general sentiment that some vacation time was beneficial to employees and, by implication, to employers. The "vacation," once the sole domain of the wealthy, gained popularity among the new middle class and eventually among manual laborers as well.

International Comparative

In Europe, France was the first country to enact legislation concerning paid time off. On June 20, 1936, the National Assembly passed a law entitling workers to "annual vacations with pay amounting to 15 days, 12 of which must be working days ... for industry and commerce and the liberal professions"[15]. The concept had a broad international appeal. In 1948, the United Nations adopted the "Universal Declaration of Human Rights" which states: Article 24 - "Everyone has the right to rest and leisure, including reasonable limitation of working hours and periodic holidays with pay"[16]. By 1984, Austria, Belgium, Canada, Denmark, Finland, West Germany, Ireland, Italy, Luxembourg, Netherlands, New Zealand, Norway, Spain and Sweden had joined France in establishing regulatory minimums for paid leave[17].

The European Social Charter, a treaty which sets standards for social and economic human rights, was adopted in 1961 by the Council of Europe. This Charter provided that member states were obliged to ensure that employers domiciled within their borders "provide for a minimum of two weeks' annual holiday with pay". In the 1996 amendment to the Charter, the annual holiday entitlement was increased from two to four weeks[18]. By 2003, the European Union adopted the "Working Time Directive" (2003/88/EC) which required EU countries to guarantee that workers will receive paid annual leave of at least four weeks per year[19]. Most countries in Europe, Africa, Asia and the Americas followed suit. As of 2012, a survey of the employment laws of 160 countries showed that only Kiribati, Laos and the U.S. had no universal statutory minimum for paid leave[20]. (See: Appendix A). Of these 160 countries, 10 percent had regulations that awarded extra time off for mothers of minor children, 28 percent for young workers, and 29 percent for older workers or workers with seniority in their jobs.

Employees in the U.S. generally spend more time working than do employees in other countries. In 1970, workers in the U.S. were at their jobs about 1,900 hours per year, a figure that was less than their counterparts in countries like Canada, France, the United Kingdom and Japan. (Only workers in Norway put in fewer hours.) Over time, this relationship reversed. By 2007, workers in each of the other countries had realized decreases the number of hours they were at their jobs while the number of hours of job attendance in the U.S. stayed relatively constant[21]. Across all OECD countries, between 1970 and 2005, the average worker's job hours declined by 3.5 percent, approximately three times the 1.3 percent decline realized in the U.S[22]. For workers in the U.S., the focus, the priorities, and the culture are distinctly different than they are elsewhere around the globe - not versus just a few affluent countries with very well-developed economies, but versus almost all other nations regardless of affluence or culture.

The Economic Argument for Vacation Time

The argument for establishing a minimum number of days or weeks for employee vacations is one that is intended to promote full employment. If a worker takes a vacation for one month each year and the business does not close for that period, a replacement worker will be needed for that time. For every twelve employees, a thirteenth worker will be needed to cover the tasks that would have been done by the people who are on leave. A similar argument was used in France in 2000 to boost job creation by reducing the official workweek from 40 to 35 hours, something that was estimated to have produced at least a short term surge in employment[23]. It is also somewhat related to the argument used by Franklin Roosevelt to create a Social Security system for older workers, namely, that taking people out of the workplace leaves room for others to come in. Interestingly, the argument for creating jobs by mandating vacation time did not become part of the "New Deal" legislation package.

In the United States, paid leave has remained unregulated. In 1938, the U.S. Congress passed the Fair Labor Standards Act (FLSA) which set standards for minimum wages and overtime pay, restricted the hours that child labor could work and prohibited child labor from engaging in certain jobs that were considered too dangerous[24], but it did not set any standard for time off for laborers, paid or unpaid. The first bill introduced to the U.S. Congress concerning paid vacations was H.R. 2564, the "Paid Vacation Act" of 2009, intended to amend the Fair Labor Standards Act to require that employers provide a minimum of one week of paid annual leave to employees. The bill was referred to the House Subcommittee on Workforce Protections and no action was taken on it. The Act was reintroduced to Congress under the same name in 2011 as H.R. 2096 and was again referred to the House Subcommittee on Workforce protections. Again, no action was taken on it.

Issues and Trends in Time Off

Time off from work is generally thought to give workers a chance to rest and recuperate and to have positive physical as well as psychological benefits[25]. These benefits largely stem from the impact the time off has on employees. The amount of time off a person takes has been shown to be positively correlated with a higher degree of happiness in his or her personal relationships with family and friends[26].

The effect on the employee's relationship with work may not be as enduring. Vacations are intended to relieve stress and to increase health and well-being, but the constancy of workflow can erode these positive effects. Prior to taking a vacation, managers and employees alike may have to prepare for their impending absence by delegating some tasks and duties to others, or by prioritizing the items to be done, doing some ahead of schedule or sequencing their steps to minimize the disruption their absences will cause[27]. This rush of activity can cause a decrease in health and well-being for one to two weeks prior to the beginning of the vacation[28]. Moreover, employees often keep in contract with work while on vacation, by phone, by text or by email, and do not fully realize the benefit of being "away."

On returning to work after a vacation, there is a parallel rush of activity with equal effect. While health and well-being have been shown to improve during a vacation, these effects fade relatively soon a vacation has ended; the lingering positive effects of the time off have been estimated to last from a week[29] to a month[30]. What does linger, however, is a fond memory of an experience. For some people, when a vacation has been a positive one, for example, a pleasant, relaxing and/or interesting trip, the vacationer will tend to be happier with his or her experience than he or she would have been had the person spent the same amount of money on a material possession, such as a better car or some other minor luxury item[31].

From an organizational point of view, time away from work represents lost productivity, and so management seeks to minimize this loss. It is the one of the most expensive of the benefits granted to workers, accounting on average for seven percent of compensation expense for the U.S. civilian labor force in 2014[32]. Having employees take paid time off is credited with lowering unwanted turnover[33], as well as with increased job satisfaction[34]. Employers tend to develop compensation and benefits packages mindful of the prevailing balance of supply and demand in the labor markets as well as on the compensation and benefits offerings of their competitors[35]. A competitive compensation package makes job switching less attractive, and so works to diminish turnover.

Other considerations include security and public image. In some industries the required absences of employees aids in fraud prevention. The work of any one employee must be handled by a substitute employee for some amount of time. For example, the Federal Deposit Insurance Corporation (FDIC) recommends that bank employees take annual vacations for uninterrupted periods of no less than two weeks[36]. Also, some organizations offer employees paid time off to participate in volunteer activities[37] or to allow them to donate their paid time off to other employees who may need them for deserving reasons[38]. These purposes can serve to augment a corporate image and improve community relations[39].

How managers and workers perceive of a paid time off benefit is associated with their respective self-images, to the roles they play in the organization and to the responsibilities they handle[40]. Managers tend to draw on a professional self-image in order to administer leave policies; they are most directly responsible for productivity, for meeting deadlines and for ensuring work flow, and they employ resources, both human and physical, to accomplish these tasks. Their priority is continuity and their goal is to minimize disruptive influences, including ones that they themselves might cause. Non-management workers tend to view time off using a relational self-conception, an understanding of themselves in relation to their families, their friends, their co-workers, etc. and view their time as allocated among these priorities. Of course, it is perhaps unfair to assume that the self-image and perceived role of any individual is this neatly defined, but the typology provides a workable basis on which to analyze the respective behaviors of managers and workers.

While paid time off is valuable to all ages within the workforce, a social trend among the more recent millennial generation shows an increasing attention to work-life balance and an emphasis on paid time off benefits[41]. This being said, the actual use of paid time off, holidays and sick days in the U.S. decreased during the 1990s[42], a trend that continued into the next two decades[43].

Access to Leave Benefits

As shown in Table 5, access to paid time off in the U.S. varies with the types of employment a person has, with his or her salary or wage level, with full or part-time status and with the type of industry in which the person is working.

Table 5

Access to Leave Benefits
U.S. Civilian Workforce - 2011
Percent of Workforce

Workforce characteristics	Percent with access to:			Avg. Hours Leave per Week
	Paid Leave	Unpaid Leave	Paid or Unpaid Leave	
Total	59.0	76.6	90.2	15.61
Occupation				
Management / Financial	77.2	72.3	92.8	15.88
Professional and related	69.4	76.2	93.0	15.97
Services	35.7	79.7	87.3	14.00
Sales and related	44.6	75.3	85.4	14.73
Office & Administrative	66.0	78.6	91.7	12.68
Construction & Extract.	36.1	71.3	84.7	n/a
Installation & Maint.	71.3	79.0	91.6	n/a
Production	62.9	81.5	90.4	20.33
Transport. & Moving	58.3	75.6	89.0	16.92
Sector				
Private, for profit	56.2	77.7	90.2	15.40
Private, not for profit	63.0	73.2	92.3	15.06
Federal government	86.3	79.2	95.7	11.02
State government	75.3	76.3	94.7	14.64
Local government	73.1	73.6	90.4	19.31
Status				
Full time	71.4	76.3	92.6	16.26
Part time	22.4	81.4	85.3	13.72
Earnings of full time workers				
$0 - $540/week	50.1	78.0	88.4	14.14
$541 - $830/week	77.1	78.9	94.7	15.77
$831 - $1,230/week	81.2	74.6	95.3	17.84
$1,231+ /week	82.8	75.4	94.9	16.47

Source: Bureau of Labor Statistics, Access to and Use of Leave – 2011: Data from the American Time Use Survey, August 16, 2012, Table 1. Note: BLS Data from 2014 does not include "unpaid" leave options.

Paid time off is more readily available to higher status and better compensated professions, to people who work on a full as opposed to a part-time basis, and to people who work in management or professional occupations as well as in union-oriented professions such as installation and maintenance (mechanical trades) or production. Further, the workers in these categories also receive more days off on average than those who are employed in the more poorly compensated positions, work part time or are in the leisure and hospitality industries. While slightly more than 70 percent of full time workers in the U.S. receive some form of paid time off, least well represented in this category (at 56 percent) are those who work in private, for-profit industries.

The U.S. stands apart from much of the rest of the world in its approach to paid time off. Almost every other nation has a law or regulation specifying the minimum number of days off with pay a full time worker must receive. In the United States, obtaining a paid time off benefit is part of an employment negotiation. For most middle class and professional occupations, this benefit is something that is fairly standard, but for retail and service workers it is not. The paid time off benefit skews to the better paying full time jobs both in terms of its absolute availability and the number of days off that are offered. Regulations that would mandate paid time off would have their greatest impact on those employed in lower wage jobs, especially those in the hospitality and retail industries.

Reasons for Taking Time Off and for Not Taking Time Off

The reasons workers take time off also varies with occupation, sector (public versus private), status (full time versus part time) and income. As shown in Table 6, while taking a vacation remains as the most cited reason for taking leave from work (29 percent), absence due to illness or to obtain some form of medical care whether for the employee or the employee's family (27.5 percent) is a very close second. Taking time off to run errands may seem like a sub-optimal use of the relatively few days off that American workers take, but it ranks third in the reasons for being absent from work.

Table 6

Main Reasons for Taking Leave
U.S. Civilian Workforce – 2011
Percent of Workforce

Workforce Characteristics	Own Illness[a]	Family Illness[b]	Child care[c]	Vaca-tion[d]	Err-and[e]	Birth of Child[f]
Total	21.9	5.6	2.3	29.5	16.5	1.7
Occupation						
Management/Fin	17.6	5.6	2.9	36.9	13.5	0.3
Professional	19.4	4.6	2.2	36.3	14.4	2.8
Services	27.6	9.0	1.1	20.2	20.5	1.1
Sales and related	21.1	1.9	3.7	35.5	15.8	3.1
Office & Admin.	24.5	4.6	1.5	25.2	17.6	1.6
Construction	n/a	n/a	n/a	n/a	n/a	n/a
Install. & Maint.	n/a	n/a	n/a	n/a	n/a	n/a
Production	22.4	2.2	2.7	33.0	19.2	0.0
Transport & Moving	30.0	3.6	3.9	12.8	21.5	1.5
Sector						
Private, for profit	20.7	5.7	2.2	28.2	17.4	1.5
Private, not for profit	28.5	5.7	2.4	33.1	11.0	5.0
Federal government	34.7	4.2	0.3	28.8	17.4	0.5
State government	25.8	7.6	1.9	26.3	14.1	2.6
Local government	21.7	4.5	3.4	38.3	13.4	1.4
Status						
Full time	22.9	5.4	2.4	30.7	14.6	2.2
Part time	17.8	6.5	1.2	27.2	20.5	0.4
Earnings of full time workers per week						
$0 - $540	30.1	5.2	4.3	19.9	17.7	2.5
$541 - $830	26.5	6.0	2.1	27.8	10.0	1.1
$831 - $1,230	21.4	5.3	0.9	31.9	16.4	1.5
$1,231+	17.1	5.3	2.0	39.4	15.0	3.8

Source: Bureau of Labor Statistics, Access to and Use of Leave – 2011: Data from the American Time Use Survey, August 16, 2012, Table 2.

Notes   a   Own illness or medical care
       b   Illness or medical care of a family member
       c   Child-care or elder-care (other than for illness)
       d   Vacation
       e   Errands or personal reasons
       f   Birth or adoption of a child

While there are differences in the patterns of time-off behavior by occupation and market sector, the largest disparity between groups of individuals can be found between those in the highest and lowest quartiles of earnings levels. Among the least affluent segment, time off is more often taken for medical reasons than for leisure, a balance that tends in the other direction for more affluent workers. One plausible explanation is that time off taken by lower income workers is more often unpaid and so its use skews to things that are practical and necessary. Note: Table 6 shows the reasons that people who are able to take time off do so; full time workers have much more access to paid time off than do part-time workers (See: Table 5).

Whether in a management or a laborer position, people who consider time off to be personally important are nearly three times more likely to use paid time off for a planned event such as a vacation than those who do not consider it to be important (34 percent versus 12 percent)[44]. The reasons employees hesitate to use their paid time off are shown in Table 7.

Four in ten employees in the U.S. use less than the amount of paid time off that they are due. Heavy workloads, an inability to delegate or share assignments, and an inability to leave work to another person's supervision describe organizational structures that are not well designed to accommodate employees taking time off. While forgoing a vacation may be a personal choice on the part of the employee, the reasons given Table 7 suggest that many people are hesitant to take time off in response to workload issues. While these may be a reflection of the level of involvement and commitment people have to their work or the pressure they feel to get their work accomplished, they may also be a symptom of poorly managed work environments.

Taken to an extreme, management may contribute to the anxieties that workers feel in scheduling time off. If a manager threatens to disallow a vacation for any reason that does not stem from a true business emergency or if the employee is not allowed to use a paid time off benefit at his or her own discretion (assuming that the timing is not otherwise disruptive to the work process, e.g., at or near key deadlines or during cyclical peaks in volume)[45], what is being created is a form of hostile work environment.

Table 7

Challenges to Taking Paid Time Off
Percent of Respondents Agreeing with the Reasons
It Is Difficult to Take Paid Time Off
2014

Very[a]	Some-what[b]	Very or Some-what[c]	Reason
12	28	40	I would come back to a mountain of work
9	26	35	No one else at my company can do the work while I'm away
11	22	33	I cannot afford a vacation
7	26	33	Taking time off is harder to do the higher you get up in a company
4	24	28	I want to show complete dedication to the company and my job
4	18	22	I don't want others to think I am replaceable
9	13	22	I can bank or roll over my unused time off
8	13	21	I get paid for my unused time off
5	15	20	I would be expected to respond to work matters and emails anyway
5	15	20	The company's culture does not promote taking time off
3	17	20	I feel guilty using my paid time off
4	15	19	I don't want to lose consideration for a promotion or pay raise
4	13	17	I would prefer to work rather than take time off
3	14	17	I am afraid of what my boss would think
4	12	16	I am afraid I would lose my job
3	12	15	Taking time off is something that comes with seniority

Source: GfK Public Affairs & Corporate Communications (July 2014). *Overwhelmed America: Why Don't We Use Our Earned Leave?*

Notes: Columns: a Very difficult
b Somewhat difficult
c Either somewhat or very difficult (a+b)

Organizations have wide discretion in determining when employees may use vacation. Provided the standards are reasonable, fair and published, the organization may require a person to arrange for paid time off at a time that will minimize any disruption to workflow, but the standards may not be applied in an arbitrary or discriminatory way. (Several states require organizations to publish or post a vacation policy.)

As stated above, employers have no obligation stemming from federal or state regulations to provide paid time off or vacation benefits to their employees; however, some states do require organizations to provide their employees with a minimum number of days off for illness. As for holidays, the Fair Labor Standards Act (FLSA) does not require organizations to pay their employees for federal or state holidays such as Independence Day, Labor Day, etc. The number of holidays or vacation days that may be taken should be specified in an employment contract, employee handbook or policy statement.

Finally, the traditional system of paid time off includes separate categories of vacation time, sick time and personal time, and each category of time off might have different rules associated with it. For example, vacation time may have to be scheduled in advance; unused vacation time may be allowed in whole or in part to be carried over to a new year, while sick time and personal time may not. By contrast, paid time off is a single category of benefit that encompasses vacation, sick and personal time and is expressed as a total number of days per year that are available to the employee for any one of these purposes.

The number of organizations that are offering paid time off has been increasing since 2000, while the number of organizations offering the traditional categories of vacation, sick and personal days has been on the decline[46]. Paid time off programs are generally easier to administer than are traditional systems and are credited with decreases in the number of unscheduled absences by employees[47]. From an employee's point of view, when operating under a paid time off program a day spent in illness marks one less day of vacation time that can be freely spent, and so taking time off for illness– usually an unscheduled day – would be seen by an employee as a loss of vacation time. The effect of using a paid time off system is that it decreases the number days of unscheduled absences that employees incur[48].

Summary

Time off from work helps people to rest and recuperate, to take care of their medical needs and those of their families, as well as to attend to errands and chores that cannot be accomplished in the evenings or on weekends and holidays. Time off benefits people in their home lives; it helps relationships, and contributes to a balance between the work and non-work aspects of a person's life. While this is important to all, it is something of particular significance to the millennial generation. While the memories of a well-enjoyed vacation can have a lasting impact on a person, the benefit of stress-relief while away from work may be short-lived. For many jobs, the rush of activity both before and after taking time off creates high levels of stress both in the anticipation of and the return from the absence.

Organizations offer time off to their employees because it increases job satisfaction and reduces turnover. In some circumstances, it helps to protect against fraud, promote a socially responsible corporate image and, in cases where employees are given time off to participate in philanthropic activities, improve community relations.

Workers in all levels of government have more access to paid time off than do workers in the private sector. Among private sector workers, access to paid time off as well as the number of vacation days to which a worker is entitled increases with total compensation as well as with employment in management, professional or industrial occupations. The U.S. is one of a very few nations that does not mandate a minimum number of days of paid time off for all full time workers. A requirement to this effect would have the greatest impact on the most poorly paid workers in the private sector.

About forty percent of the workers in the U.S. do not take all of the paid time off to which they are entitled. Much of the reason for this stems from work pressures. Fear of the work that would be amassed while a person is taking time off - often compounded because there are no immediately available resources to cover the tasks while a person is away - are the chief contributors to this pressure. If management or colleagues contribute to this pressure, this situation is more than just badly managed; it can rise to the level of a hostile work environment.

Organizations have begun switching from offering time off in categories – vacation, personal days, sick days – to offering an undifferentiated paid time off. This has the effect of reducing unplanned absences from work, as sick days are usually taken on little notice. Under this system, taking sick days erodes the total time off available to employees and so it appears to the worker as a loss of vacation time.

5 HEALTH CARE

"All were in good health. One could not use the word
ill-health in connection with the symptoms
Ivan Ilyitch sometimes complained of…"

Leo Tolstoy
The Death of Ivan Ilyitch (1886)

Background

Health care is the maintenance and improvement of physical and mental health through the provision of medical services. Health insurance is intended to assist in paying for these services. Under the Patient Protection and Affordable Care Act of 2010, health insurance plans must cover outpatient surgery, emergency services, hospitalization, maternity and newborn care, mental health and substance abuse services, rehabilitative services and devices, laboratory services, preventative and wellness services, chronic disease management and pediatric services[1].

Plans may have deductibles, copays and coinsurance. A deductible is the amount an insured person must pay each calendar year before the insurance company begins to contribute to his or her medical expenses. A copay is a flat dollar amount that must be paid each time a service is used;

for example, there may be a $20 charge each time a person visits a physician. Coinsurance is the percentage of the cost of medical care that an insured person must pay; on average, people who have medical insurance through their work in the U.S. pay 20 percent of the cost of medical care (30 percent of the cost of the care when it is extended to the insured's family)[2].

A History of Health Care Benefits

Health insurance in the U.S. can be traced back nearly to the beginning of the country itself. In 1798, the 5th Congress passed the "Act for the Relief of Sick and Disabled Seamen"[3] which established a network of hospitals for the care of merchant seamen. In 1847 the Massachusetts Health Insurance Company of Boston sold insurance policies covering accidental injuries or death[4], a type of insurance that would later expand to cover losses stemming from illnesses as well. During the Progressive Era (1890 – 1920), these policies were termed "sickness insurance" and were used to cover the lost wages of people who missed work. (In 1911, the National Insurance Act was passed in Great Britain recasting the term "sickness insurance" with a more optimistic title: "health insurance"; the term was adopted in America shortly thereafter.) At the time, health care costs were relatively modest; people were treated for their injuries and illnesses in their own homes into the 1920s[5]. The most significant economic consequence of sickness or injury was lost income.

At the beginning of the 20th century, medical practices started to become more complex and comprehensive and the treatment of accidents and diseases, while gaining in effectiveness, also increased in cost. Largely because of advances in the study of germs and contagions, treatments migrated out of homes and into health centers[6]. The American Medical Association, which was founded in 1847, began to develop licensing standards and to set educational requirements for those training in the medical professions[7]. Medical expense insurance developed in response to the increasing cost of health care.

In 1929, Justin Ford Kimball, working as the vice president of the Baylor University Medical Center, noticed that the hospital had a large number of unpaid bills -- many of which were from area teachers. Based on plans then in use by companies in the railroad and lumber industries, he developed a system for teachers in the Dallas area to collectively pre-pay for a hospital stay, should it be needed. More than three quarters of the area teachers enrolled in the plan. Based on its initial success, the American Hospital Association (AHA) promoted the concept to its members. Eventually, similar plans were offered by individual hospitals and community health care organizations and these, with the help of the AHA, joined to form a single organization under the name of Blue Cross[8]. Ten years later, physicians who were not affiliated with hospitals also organized their own prepayment plans which came together under the name Blue Shield.

Government-Backed Programs

In 1883, Germany, under the leadership of Otto Von Bismarck, was the first nation to initiate a "Social Health Insurance" system, a system that began modestly and expanded incrementally over the next century to include a growing list of protected classes until the coverage eventually became universal[9]. Other nations followed. In 1937, the Soviet Union implemented a universal health care system[10], followed by New Zealand in 1939 to 1941, and the United Kingdom in 1948. Other nations, including Sweden, Iceland, Norway, Denmark, Finland, Japan, Canada, Australia, Italy, Portugal, Greece, and Spain followed over the next five decades.

In the United States, universal health care was first proposed by President Theodore Roosevelt, a second time by President Franklin D. Roosevelt (the Wagner National Health Act of 1939), and a third time by President Harry Truman as part of the "Fair Deal" program. Each time the U.S. Congress considered this concept, resistance to it swelled chiefly for two reasons. One was that Congress had a hesitancy to implement any system that had socialist overtones. Second was that the American Medical Association, concerned that universal health care would lead to the regulation of care including restrictions on the choice of physician as well as to constraints on the method and amounts of payment, was steadfastly opposed to the concept[11].

In the meanwhile, private employers also began to address issues of health coverage. The Traveler's Insurance Company began offering accident insurance in 1863; Traveler's along with the Aetna Life Insurance Company offered health insurance as early as 1899. During the 1870s and 1880s, companies that employed workers in hazardous professions as could be found in the mining, lumber and railroad industries offered plans to cover medical services. In 1910, Montgomery Ward and Company became the first institution to offer health insurance to all of its general employees as a job benefit[12]. The concept grew slowly. By 1940, a little less than ten percent of the population of the U.S. was covered by some form of health insurance and half of that number consisted of enrollment in a Blue Cross/Blue Shield plan[13].

During World War II, a labor shortage began to drive up the cost of wages. Concerned that inflation would have a detrimental effect on the U.S. economy, Congress passed the Stabilization Act of 1942 which authorized President Roosevelt to freeze wages at their then-current levels. The Act provided for two exceptions, namely, "insurance and pension benefits in a reasonable amount to be determined by the President"[14]. While employers were not able to attract workers by offering wage increases, they were able to offer more appealing total compensation packages by including insurance and pension benefits. These benefits packages spread quickly and by 1950 approximately one half of the U.S. population was covered by some form of health care insurance[15]. Helping this movement even further, in 1954 the Internal Revenue Code was amended to exempt employer as well as employee contributions to health plans from taxes[16].

While resistance to a comprehensive national health care system remained throughout the next several decades, the focus of discussions on the topic gradually shifted away from how to promote the purchase of health insurance by companies for their employees to how to provide health care for those who were unlikely to obtain jobs with benefits – those who lived at or near the poverty line, as well as children and the elderly[17]. In 1965, Congress enacted Medicare, which provides compulsory insurance for people aged 65 and over, and Medicaid, which provides care for low-income people. Congress passed the Mental Health Parity Act in 1996, which boosted psychiatric benefits and the Children's Health Insurance

Program in 1997, which provides health care assistance to low-income children.

In 2010, the Patient Protection and Affordable Care Act was signed into law by President Barack Obama. Its purpose was to make health care insurance compulsory for all U.S. citizens and to provide access to insurance for those people who were not otherwise covered by employment-based health plans, by Medicare, Medicaid or any other alternative program. For lower and middle income families, tax subsidies were designed to assist in paying for the care. Under this Act, health care coverage will become a mandatory work benefit for medium to large firms by 2016.

Recent Developments in Health Care

As of 2013, about 86.6 percent of the U.S. population was covered by some form of health care insurance. Employer-sponsored health insurance covered approximately 169 million non-elderly people in the US, or about 53.9 percent of the total population. Other sources included insurance that was directly purchased by consumers (11.0 percent of the population), Medicare (15.6 percent), Medicaid (17.3 percent) and Military Health Care (4.5 percent)[18]. The percentages of insurance by source do not add to the 86.6 percent coverage number because people often have multiple insurance plans and use one as a primary plan and a second as a supplementary one.

The uninsured portion of the U.S. population tends to be concentrated among young adults, aged 21 to 34, and among people who were employed on a part-time rather than full-time basis. It is highest among the poor and working-poor segments of the population[19]. Participation in some form of insurance coverage increases with age and income[20].

Employers generally require that their employees make some contribution toward the cost of their health insurance. On average, workers who participate in an insurance plan pay 18 percent of the total cost of the premiums of individual plans and 29 percent of the cost of family plans. Between 2003 and 2013, the cost of family coverage increased by approximately 80 percent, but the relative portions paid by employers and employees have remained the same, that is, employees have absorbed 29 percent of the increase and employers have absorbed the remainder[21].

Through 2014, access to employer-based health insurance benefits was highest among teachers, union members, managers and financial executives; access to health benefits was lowest among workers in service trades, among part-time employees[22] and among those employed in construction and retail trade[23]. Access to employer-based health insurance also varied by firm size; slightly more than half of firms with one to 49 employees offered health care benefits but more than 90 percent of firms with 500 or more employees offered health care benefits to their employees[24].

Issues and Trends in Health Care

Health care is offered as a job benefit because it helps with recruitment and retention, and it increases productivity by reducing absenteeism and turnover[25]. For employees, health care is perceived as an important benefit, but even though employers who offer health care as a benefit subsidize approximately 80 percent of its cost, people who use these services tend to be sensitive to prices[26]. Consumers of health care services are often asked to contribute toward their initial costs – a "deductible" amount – before insurance benefits begin to subsidize the care. Increasing the amount of a deductible inhibits the initial usage of health care services[27]. Avoiding the high cost of medical services in the U.S. is the principal reason that medical tourism has become popular[28].

The free market system of the U.S. healthcare industry provides citizens with uneven access to medical services. Uninsured adults have less access to medical care than do insured adults, they receive a poorer quality of care when they do obtain it, and they generally experience worse health outcomes than do insured adults[29]. Basing health care coverage on employment creates a circular problem. Health conditions that prevent people from working or from working on a full-time basis can restrict their access to health insurance[30]. The Affordable Care Act, which mandates the purchase of health insurance, helps to make it available to people who are unemployed or who are employed on a part-time basis and do not have a health care benefit, but still carries with it an out-of-pocket expense. Further, employer sponsored plans provide a pre-tax benefit for employees and are deductible expenses for employers; health insurance purchased by individuals is only deductible to the extent their expenses, together with all of the other medical expenses an individual may have during a year, exceed a threshold of ten percent of a taxpayer's adjusted gross income[31]. For most uninsured workers, health insurance costs will not be deductible.

Access to health care benefits declined between 1991 and 2002, coincident with an increase in the percentage of the U.S. population that was employed on a part-time versus full-time basis. Between 2003 and 2012, access to and participation in health care benefits continued to decline in the U.S. for several reasons: a growth in the non-union labor force, in part-time work, in lower wage work and in the percentage of jobs available through small establishments[32]. Non-union jobs as well as part-time jobs have lower offering rates of health care benefits than do union-based and full-time jobs[33], and higher paying jobs more frequently carry health care benefits than do lower wage jobs[34]. Further, smaller firms are less likely to offer health benefits than are larger firms[35, 36].

Under key provisions of the Affordable Care Act, beginning in 2015, organizations with 100 or more employees will have to pay a penalty if they do not offer adequate and affordable health care coverage to their employees, a provision that is scheduled to be extended to organizations with 50 or more employees in 2016[37].

Prior to the enactment of the Affordable Care Act, insurance companies had the option to avoid paying for expenses associated with the "prior existing conditions" of new enrollees. Because much health insurance was employment-based, people who had illnesses, injuries or other medical conditions, especially ones that were expensive to manage and treat[38], were reluctant to change jobs as a new job meant new insurance coverage that would not pay for the treatment of these conditions. While several attempts had been made to address this issue prior to the adoption of the Affordable Care Act, none were particularly effective. The adoption of the Health Insurance Portability and Accountability Act in 1996, for example, was intended to enable workers to carry the insurance they had obtained through an employer with them for eighteen months after they became unemployed or moved to a new job, but it did so only if the worker paid the entire cost of the coverage. On average, employers pay approximately 80 percent of the cost of health insurance, and so continuing coverage under an ex-employer's plan could be quite expensive. As of January 1, 2014, the Affordable Care Act[39] provided that prior existing conditions cannot be used to deny coverage to people, nor can they be used as a reason for increasing the cost of insurance to any one individual.

Consumer Directed Health Plans

Consumer directed health plans (CDHPs) were introduced in the early 1990s to help contain the growing cost of health care for employees[40,41]. These health plans shift the responsibility for determining the type of care that a consumer receives from the insurer to the beneficiary. The plans typically have three features: a high deductible; a personal spending account; and the availability of information on treatments[42]. In theory, this shift in responsibility should work to stabilize health care costs by making health care decision subject to the normalizing influences of supply and demand[43]. To make this work, consumers have to be informed of the probable effectiveness of available treatment programs as well as their potential costs[44].

While the specific terms of CDHPs may vary, there are two common structures which these plans follow. Health Reimbursement Arrangements (HRAs) were qualified as deductible benefit expenses by the Internal Revenue Service in 2002; these are employee-specific accounts established and funded by an employer from which an employee can be reimbursed for medical expenses and which can be excluded from the taxable income of the employee[45]. Health Savings Accounts (HSAs), by contrast, are established and funded by individuals. Contributions by individuals to these accounts were made deductible for personal income tax purposes by the Medicare Prescription Drug Improvement and Modernization Act of 2003[46].

Advocates of CDHPs argue that consumer involvement in medical treatment decisions accommodates consumer preferences and avoids perpetrating the perception that managed care plans were limiting access to potentially beneficial care[47]. In general, health plan choices are influenced by premium levels, deductible and coinsurance payments, and the structure of tiered formulas. Age, gender, marital status and compensation level also influence the types of coverage choices people make[48]. Involving consumers in their own health care decisions assumes that these consumers are well informed but price-conscious and that they will be able to make decisions uninfluenced by the organizations with which they are affiliated[49]. The assumption that consumers are well-enough informed, however, may not be universally true. Decisions about the best medical treatment to follow may require a deeper understanding of the effectiveness of the available options than the average consumer is likely to have[50].

People who are enrolled in CDHPs use their benefits differently than do those who are enrolled in managed care programs. Enrollees in CDHP plans were more likely than those in managed care programs to seek and use medical information and to forgo medical treatments in order to save money[51]. Further, consumers tend to be price sensitive to out-of-pocket costs for treatments, a phenomenon that is especially pronounced among younger, healthier individuals[52]. The behavioral differences of people enrolled in CDHPs versus those enrolled in managed care programs give rise to concerns that consumers may not be effectively evaluating the cost/benefit tradeoffs of treatment options and may be reducing the quality of their care in order to save money, a trade-off that may skew with its most negative effects on low-income or less healthy users[53].

CDHPs were adopted by organizations to help keep their health care plan costs contained, and have effectively reduced the cost of providing this benefit to their employees[54]. By involving consumers in their medical treatment decisions, users of these programs are becoming more informed about their medical treatment options as well as about the conditions that they may have[55]. One of the collateral impacts of learning about treatments and health in general is that more than half of the enrollees in CDHP programs reported that they felt that their knowledge of health care management increased and more than a quarter of these enrollees reported improved behaviors[56].

Table 8

Access to Health Benefits / Employer Share of Premium
U.S. Civilian Workforce – 2014
Percent of Workforce

| | Private Industry | | | State & Local Government | | |
| | | Employer Share of Premium | | | Employer Share of Premium | |
	Access to	Em-ployee	Fam-ily	Access to	Em-ployee	Fam-ily
Total	69	79	68	87	87	71
Occupation						
Management/Finan.	87	79	69	n/a	n/a	n/a
Professional/related	95	81	71	89	87	69
Services	40	77	62	81	87	73
Sales and related	71	73	63	n/a	n/a	n/a
Office & Admin.	77	79	68	84	88	72
Construction & Maint.	76	79	67	95	88	73
Production & Trans.	76	79	72	81	87	72
Size of Firm						
1 to 49 workers	53	79	62	65	92	73
50 to 99 workers	69	77	63	87	91	69
100 to 499 workers	80	78	70	86	88	69
500 workers or more	89	80	76	90	87	71
Status						
Full time	86	86	69	99	87	71
Part time	23	78	63	24	88	69
Earnings of full time workers						
Lowest 10 percent	20	70	57	53	89	56
Lowest 25 percent	34	74	58	68	87	63
Second 25 percent	74	78	66	92	88	73
Third 25 percent	86	79	70	94	88	71
Highest 25 percent	93	81	72	97	87	74
Highest 10 percent	94	81	72	97	88	79

Source: Bureau of Labor Statistics, Economic News Release, July 25, 2014
Table 3: Medical Plans, Access, Participation, and Take-up Rates.

An additional development in medical care is the emergence of concierge medical services, those that establish a relationship between a patient and a primary care physician in which the patient pays an annual fee or retainer. In exchange for this fee, patients receive same day or next day appointments for non-urgent care, access to a primary care physician 24 hours a day and preventive medical services not usually offered through managed care or other common health insurance plans[57]. There is a risk that patients may overuse health care services because a flat fee entitles them to unlimited visits to a physician even if the visits are not medically necessary[58], but for those patients who do need extra attention because of an illness or impairment, the added service may be vital. While the percentage of companies in the U.S. offering CDHP plans exceeds 50 percent[69], the percent of people with employer-sponsored health insurance who were enrolled in a CDHP only grew from 4 percent in 2006 to 18 percent in 2013[60]. Acceptance of these types of health care plans is growing, but remains guarded.

As shown in Table 8, through 2014, health benefits were much more accessible to those who were working full time rather than part time, and to those who were working in professional or managerial positions than to those who were working in lower wage jobs in the service industries. Larger firms also tended to offer the benefit more frequently than did smaller firms. By contrast, state and local governments offered health benefits at a relatively uniform rate in spite of the compensation level of their employees.

Summary

The growth of employer-sponsored health care benefits has been strongly influenced by federal government policy and regulation. Organizations first began offering health care and insurance benefits to those employed in several especially hazardous trades to replace lost wages in case of death or severe physical injury. Over time, health care became the most commonly offered benefit among large organizations in the U.S.; legislation enacted during World War II encouraged organizations to offer health care benefits and resulted in their widespread acceptance. In 2014, approximately 54 percent of the population of the U.S. was covered by an employer-sponsored health care program, a number that can be expected to increase as a result of the passage of the Affordable Care Act.

Employer-sponsored health care programs are deductible expenses for the sponsoring organization. When employees contribute to these programs, whether through deductions from their gross pay or by contributions to medical spending accounts, the amounts contributed are not included in employee income for tax purposes. When an employee pays for his or her own medical insurance, the cost of the insurance is only deductible to the extent his or her total annual medical expenses exceeds a threshold income (currently 10 percent of Adjusted Gross Income). The tax benefit afforded to organizations and to employees of organizations acts as a partial government subsidy for health care programs provided through employers.

For the last several decades, organizations and employees alike have coped with rising health care costs. During the recession of 2007 through 2011, a decrease in full-time employment was offset to a limited extent by a rise in part-time work. Because benefits are granted to part-time employees less often than they are to full-time employees, fewer people had health care coverage during this time. Also, organizations have begun to promote consumer-directed health plans (CDHPs) as opposed to managed care options to their employees.

CDHPs put the primary responsibility for making health care purchasing decisions on consumers of these services who spend pre-tax funds allocated to health reimbursement or savings accounts for this purpose. As consumers tend to be more price-sensitive when spending their own funds, the consumer-directed aspect of these plans has helped to slow the growth in health care costs. In order for CDHPs to be effective, however, consumers of health care services need access to information about the cost and effectiveness of available treatments.

6 FAMILY AND MEDICAL LEAVE

"Nora: Why did you marry him then?
Mrs. Linde: Well, you see – Mother was still alive;
she was bedridden; completely helpless;
and I had my two younger brothers to take care of.
I didn't think it would be right to refuse him."

Henrik Ibsen
A Doll's House (1879)

Background

When the Family and Medical Leave Act (FMLA) of 1993 was first being considered, it was the subject of much debate and controversy and did not pass easily into law. Its legislative history demonstrates the thresholds that initiatives in labor legislation must overcome. It also demonstrates how the arguments for and against labor legislation are framed. In all, nearly eight years passed between the time when the legislation was first introduced to Congress and when it was signed into law.

The first introduction of FMLA legislation to the House of Representatives was made by Rep. Patricia Schroeder, et al. on April 4, 1985 as H.R. 2020, the Parental and Disability Leave Act of 1985. The bill, which provided that employees would be eligible for 18 weeks of unpaid parental leave over a 24-month period for the birth, adoption, or serious illness of a child, and 26 weeks of unpaid leave over a 12-month period for an employee's own serious health condition, was intended to apply to businesses employing five or more people[1]. The bill was referred to the Committee on Education and Labor, and, in turn to its subcommittees on Labor-Management Relations and Labor Standards, as well as to the Committee on the Post Office and Civil Service, and its subcommittees on Civil Service and on Compensation and Employee Benefits. The bill emerged from each of these committees and was presented to the First Joint House Oversight Hearings on the issue of parental and disability leave on October 17, 1985; however, the Joint House Committee did not take action on the bill in time for it to be presented to the 98th session of the full Congress[2]. Bills that are not voted into law during a session of Congress are not held over to subsequent sessions and must be introduced anew in the following year if the sponsor(s) intends to pursue their passage.

A version of the bill was introduced to Congress in 1986 where it passed through the same four House subcommittees and was entered onto the agenda of the House, but the 99th Congress was adjourned before any action was taken[3]. Similarly, in 1987, the bill was presented to the House[4], and was introduced to the Senate at the same time[5]. While the same four House subcommittees again approved the bill and brought it to the floor of the House, the Senate referred the bill to its Committee on Labor and Human Resources which delegated it to the Subcommittee on Children, Families, Drugs and Alcoholism. The Subcommittee held a series of hearings in Los Angeles, Chicago, Atlanta and Washington, D.C. throughout 1987 and 1988[6]. The bill was reported out of the Senate Committee on Labor and Human Resources on September 26, 1988 and was filibustered when brought to the floor[7]. The Senate failed to end the filibuster by a cloture vote (a motion or process in parliamentary procedure used to bring debate to a quick end) of 50 to 46.

The bill was re-introduced on February 2, 1989 to both the House and the Senate[8]. In the House, the bill was modified to cover employees for up to 12 weeks of unpaid leave per year, the exemption for small employers was raised to 50 employees, and the coverage of family leave was extended to spouses with serious health conditions[9]. The bill was brought to the floor of the House for a vote on May 10, 1990, where it passed by a margin of 237 to 187[10]. On June 14, 1990, the bill was approved by the Senate by unanimous consent[11]. The bill was then presented to President George Bush on June 29, 1990 and was vetoed[12].

On January 3, 1991, a bill with wording identical to that vetoed by President George Bush was introduced to both the House and Senate[13]. With minor modifications -- certain notice and eligibility requirements were edited in the Senate version – the Senate approved the bill on October 2, 1991 by a vote of 65 to 32[14]. The House version of the bill was amended to include the changes proposed by the Senate and passed by a vote of 253 to 177 on November 13th of that year. The bills that were passed in the House and the Senate contained some minor language differences and so they were brought to the House-Senate Conference Committee for re-drafting. The Conference Committee produced a unified version of the bill which was passed by the Senate on August 11, 1992, and a month later by the House on September 10th[15].

On September 22, 1992, President Bush again vetoed the bill[16]. The Senate overrode the veto on September 24 by a vote of 68 to 31, but the House narrowly failed to do so by a vote of 258 to 169, 24 votes less than the required two-thirds majority[17].

The bill was reintroduced to the House and the Senate in 1993[18] and Labor Secretary Robert Reich testified in favor of the bill before the Senate Subcommittee on Children, Families, Drugs and Alcoholism[19]. On February 4, 1993, the bill passed the House by a vote of 247 to 152 and, on the same day, passed the Senate by a vote of 71 to 25[20]. The bill was signed into law by President Bill Clinton on February 5, 1993 and became effective on August 5th of that year.

Arguments For and Against the FMLA

The bill had been opposed in part because it was viewed by some as not being in the best interests of business. One of the compromises made to the early version of the bill, which had been intended to cover organizations with five or more people, was that the final version of the bill increased that threshold to organizations of 50 people or more. The impact of this change was to exclude 95 percent of all businesses and from 40 to 50 percent of all U.S. employees from coverage[21].

Mandated requirements for leave were viewed as a "direct intrusion by the Federal Government into the free market" and an interference with an employer's right to freely negotiate with and create a contract with an employee[22]. Other critics argued that the then proposed legislation would create a "one size fits all benefit" that would be more utilized by the upper and wealthier classes than the poorer ones who could not afford to take unpaid leave[23]. In presenting the same point to the House, Rep. Woolsey argued that two-thirds of employees who need to take family leave would not because they simply could not afford to give up the income[24].

A key argument against the bill was that it had the potential of producing a discriminatory impact on some employees in favor of others who may not want the benefit, but would have to pay for it either through taxes or an unwanted reallocation of work[25]. The argument assumes that the average work environment is time-based and gendered. The time-based aspect of the argument is premised on the concept that a simple linear relationship exists between time and productivity, on the long term shift in employment contracts in the U.S. from hourly to salary-based compensation, and on the common practice of costing benefits on a per capita rather than a per-hour-worked basis[26].

The FMLA, while conferring a very specific set of rights for employees under clearly enumerated conditions, must still be evaluated within the institutional settings of employers[27]. The FMLA created a minimum labor standard that recognized that family and medical emergencies can take a priority over work under certain circumstances and established that employees may need at times to balance their family and job responsibilities[28]. In short, it recognizes that non-work, family events can have an impact on the workplace, and mandates that employers accommodate them[29].

Extending this concept beyond the terms of the FMLA has met with limited acceptance. Title VII of the Civil Rights Act of 1964 forbids employers from discriminating against any individual in the hiring or firing of that person, or in any way that might adversely affect that person's status as an employee because of race, color, religion, sex or national origin[30], but the treatment of "sex" as the basis for discrimination has been uneven.

In Phillips v. Martin Marietta Corp., an action brought under Title VII, the U.S. Supreme Court found that when mothers of pre-school aged children were not being hired but men within the same category were being hired, a prima facie case of bias against women was presented[31]. More recent cases, however, have not been based on "sex discrimination" as defined by Title VII – the lack of access to employment or the equal treatment of employees; rather, these cases have used arguments that employees must be able to meet the requirements of their institutional settings. When primary caregivers were unable to meet the demands of a workplace that did not offer time-based flexibility, the decision by workers not to stay with the employer was characterized as a worker "choice"[32]. In 1997, the Massachusetts Supreme Court affirmed an employee's termination for her refusal to work overtime when her refusal was based on her asserted need to meet her family caregiving obligations[33]. The requirement that a person must be "available for work" has been interpreted in many states to mean that the person requesting reinstatement in his or her position be available for work on a full-time basis, regardless of the flexibility or inflexibility of the hours of the position[34].

Also, prior to the enactment of the FMLA, the U.S. Supreme Court took the position that discrimination on the basis of pregnancy was not a violation of Title VII of the Civil Rights Act[35]. It was in part in response to this decision that Congress passed the Pregnancy Discrimination Act of 1978, which amended Title VII to include expectant mothers[36]. The enactment of this legislation produced a backlash which took shape in the case of California Federal Savings & Loan Association v. Guerra (1987)[37]. In this case, state legislation granting maternity leave was challenged as inconsistent with the Pregnancy Discrimination Act; the plaintiff challenged the law as providing special treatment for women. Feminist advocates were divided, arguing that pregnant women should be treated equally with men or, alternately, that they should receive special treatment given their biological status[38]. The conflict was resolved by the Court extending "paternity" benefits to men that were similar to those being offered to mothers with new-born infants.

The arguments over whether and to what extent accommodations in working hours should be extended to those who are pregnant or take maternity leave have shown little sign of abatement. In August, 2011, the U.S. District Court for the Southern District of New York rendered its decision in the case of the EEOC v. Bloomberg[39]. The court granted the defendant's motion for summary judgment in finding that there was insufficient evidence to determine that the defendant had participated in a systemized practice of discrimination against pregnant women or women who had taken maternity leave. The court asserted that the Pregnancy Discrimination Act does not require the creation of special programs for women, and further, that the plaintiff must demonstrate that the pattern of discrimination was both intentional and part of the defendant's "standard operating procedure"[40]. The Court explained its position by referring to a speech that former General Electric CEO Jack Welch had made before the Society for Human Resource Management on June 28, 2009 as recounted in the Wall Street Journal. Mr. Welch was quoted as saying, "There's no such thing as work-life balance. There are work-life choices, and you make them, and they have consequences."[41]. The Court reiterated this sentiment in its conclusion when it stated that "... it is not the Court's role to engage in policy debates or choose the outcome it thinks best. It is to apply the law. The law does not mandate 'work-life balance.'"[42].

Issues and Trends Concerning the FMLA

The Family and Medical Leave Act of 1993 entitles workers to take up to 12 weeks of unpaid leave for the birth or adoption of a child, or to care for a "serious health condition" of their own, or that of a parent, spouse, or child[43]. The benefits provided by this law may be used in tandem with accrued vacation time or medical leave that may be available to workers while during hospital stays or otherwise under medical care.

The passage of the FMLA was premised on the assumption that a "direct correlation exists between stability in the family and productivity in the workplace"[44]. Eligible employees were those who had been employed for at least one year and had completed at least 1,250 hours of service in the 12 months immediately preceding the request for leave[45]. Also, the law covers only those firms that employ 50 people or more[46]. Provided these conditions are met, the employee may request and must be granted up to twelve weeks of unpaid leave in any one twelve month period[47]. On returning to work, the employee is entitled to be restored to the position that he or she had left for the leave, or to a position equivalent in pay, benefits and other terms and conditions[48].

Because the law covers only those firms that employ 50 or more people, it was estimated that it applied to only 11 percent of the firms in the U.S. and 46.5 percent of the workforce[49]. Covered workers tend to have higher levels of education and higher incomes than those who are not eligible for FMLA leave[50]. Note: California, Rhode Island and New Jersey provide exceptions to the general rule that family and medical leave can be "unpaid". The California Family Rights Act of 1990 allowed citizens of that state to file claims for unemployment compensation while on the unpaid leave permitted by the FMLA[51]. Despite these limitations, the passage of the FMLA codified the practice of place-holding jobs for people who take leave under the specified family caregiving circumstances and ensured that its protections were uniformly available to employees of larger firms nationwide.

International Comparative

In comparison to maternity benefits offered in other countries, those offered in the U.S. are relatively low. Of the 167 countries whose maternity benefits were tracked by the International Labour Organization (ILO), only Papua New Guinea and the U.S. did not provide some form of cash benefit to women on maternity leave[52]. (See Appendix B). The focus of the ILO approach to maternity benefits was "to ensure that women's work does not pose risks to the health of the woman and her child and to ensure that women's reproductive roles do not compromise their economic and employment security[53]." By contrast, the premise of the FMLA was that "a direct correlation exists between stability in the family and productivity in the workplace[54]." The International Labour Organization's statement focuses on the health and security of the individual; the intent of the FMLA is to stabilize the family environment at a critical juncture in the family's growth, and in doing so, reap a benefit for businesses. While the FMLA addressed the conditions surrounding the birth or adoption of an infant or a medical emergency of an immediate family member, it was not intended to provide a long term aid for the conflicts inherent in parenting and work.

From an employee's perspective, one of the major disadvantages of the FMLA is the lack of wage replacement for those who take the leave[55]. The absence of a cash benefit attendant to family leave increases the incidence of upper-income (as opposed to lower-income) mothers eventually returning to work to resume their pre-birth jobs[56]. Females who are unmarried and have an income of less than $35K/year are generally less eligible for FMLA benefits than their more affluent counterparts, and even when they are eligible for them, tend to take advantage of these benefits less often[57]. In practice, then, the FMLA works more strongly to the benefit of upper income rather than lower income workers. The prediction of Rep. Woolsey that two-thirds of employees who need to take family leave would not because they simply could not afford to give up their income has in large part been realized.

Summary

The Family and Medical Leave Act was perhaps first conceived as social legislation, but its preamble and intent statement indicate that it was passed as something that would be a benefit to business, a source of economic stimulus and stability. The lack of a cash benefit for workers who qualify for the benefits conferred by the Act has two salient characteristics: One, it separates the U.S. from almost every other country in the level and kind of benefits that pertain to the birth or adoption of a child or family medical emergencies. Two, it imbues the benefit with a bias toward the more affluent workers.

The process of enacting the FMLA was a long and arduous one, taking nearly eight years from the time it was first introduced to Congress to the time that it became law. It passed through dozens of Congressional committees and subcommittees and survived a Senate filibuster and two presidential vetoes. At the end of these debates the FMLA was passed and labor in the U.S. has since been afforded a level of family and medical leave protection that is somewhat less than the international standard.

The International Labour Organization (ILO) adopted its first convention concerning maternity protection in 1919 (No. 3) which provided that women should not be terminated from their employment in connection with the immediate period before and after the birth of a child[58]. The ILO adopted two further conventions: The Maternity Protection Convention (No. 183) in 2000, providing that maternity leave and cash benefits in case of maternity should be officially recognized as a key component of social security as established by the Social Security (Minimum Standards) Convention, 1952 (No. 102), and a recommendation (No. 202) that lists maternity benefits as part of the basic social security guarantees that should be the rights of citizens – including access to health care, maternity leave and income security[59]. The organization considers maternity protection a fundamental human right.

7 FLEXIBLE WORK OPTIONS

"It was very odd to these two persons,
who knew each other passing well,
that the mere circumstance of meeting in a new place and in a new way
should make them so awkward and constrained."

Thomas Hardy
Far from the Madding Crowd (1874)

Background

In the early 1960s, West Germany was experiencing a labor shortage. At the time, German women had not traditionally engaged in work outside the home and organizations were beginning to consider ways to attract them, but there were several obstacles. One was that female engagement in the labor force would represent something of a cultural shift from what was understood to be the proper gender roles of the population. Two was that the normal work-day schedule of 9:00am to 5:00pm shifts caused scheduling conflicts. Children might have to be brought to or picked up from school; family members might have medical appointments, etc. Whether it was the male or the female in the household who attended to these responsibilities, someone had to be present for them and not be at work during the normal business day.

In 1965, Christel Kammerer[1], a consultant and political economist, published an article proposing that Gleitzeit (translated: sliding time) or what has come to be known as flextime could be used to solve this problem and boost female employment. The concept was straightforward: A worker could have the flexibility to both start and end work at earlier times than normal, or alternately start and end at later times. A worker might even to take a break during the day, resume work and finish late. As long as the expected hours of work were met, the time of the day in which they were accomplished could be moved.

Two years later, the Messerschmidt Research and Development Company located outside of Munich, Germany was looking for a way to handle a different kind of scheduling problem. At the time, the company employed approximately 14,000 workers at its Munich facility and access to the company's parking lot was by means of a single two-lane road. Traffic jams created a problem with tardiness in the mornings and frustration in the evenings. The company hired Ms. Kammerer to help work out a system allowing workers to arrive and leave early or to arrive and leave late to help solve this problem. At first, the new Gleitzeit practice was tested on a small fraction of the workforce but it proved to be a very popular and effective solution and was soon made available to the entire workforce. Congestion decreased, employee morale increased, and, interestingly, the company began to attract female workers.

The practice of flextime spread quickly across Europe and came to the U.S. in 1973. By 1975, an estimated one million workers in the U.S. were using some form of flexible scheduling[2]. By 2011, more than half of the businesses in the U.S. offered flextime as a benefit to their employees[3].

Flextime and Compressed Work Weeks

Flexible work arrangements help both employers and employees. As for employees, flexible work arrangements have been shown to decrease work-related illnesses[4], to lower stress and to result in better health and well-being over time[5]. Employees who have access to flexible working arrangements that are supported by management have higher levels of job satisfaction[6] and job commitment[7].

Compressed workweeks are schedules that allow an employee to work a 35 or a 40 hour workweek in less than the traditional five days. For example, a full-time employee may complete the expected 40 hours for a week by working for four 10-hour days rather than five 8-hour days. This is a form of flextime and, from an employee perspective, has many of the same outcomes. It may not be an optimal solution for parents who have to bring children to school and pick them up later in the day, but it can work well for a single individual who is pursuing advanced education or for a divorced parent whose primary childcare responsibility is on a weekend.

The use of flextime can also have a positive impact on an employee's work-life balance as it helps a person to engage more fully in personal life activities. Scheduling becomes easier. For example, if a child or an elder person in an employee's care needs to be accompanied on a medical appointment, an employee who has a flexible work schedule can do this without having to use vacation time. Flextime is even more beneficial at times when work demands are high. It can buffer the adverse effect of a tight schedule by allowing an employee to allocate his or her time efficiently among work and non-work tasks[8]. As with flextime, a compressed workweek is also effective at reducing work-life stress especially in periods of high work demand[9].

A secondary impact of making the most efficient use of time is that it can enable a person to allocate some personal time for activities such as reading, entertainment, hobbies and social activities, without which people tend to have increased stress levels[10]. When work demands consume extra time, necessary non-work activities such as shopping, cleaning, etc. tend to get compressed into the shorter hours that are available to the employee, and time for personal and social activities tends to get sacrificed. (Alternately, personal and social activities may be a person's priority rather than shopping, cleaning, etc.). The same tendency to feel increased stress that can develop from having a lack of personal time can also develop when clear work/non-work boundaries are not kept. Without designating weekends or other definite blocks of time for personal and social activities, people are susceptible to feeling an imbalance in the relative amounts of time they spend and thought they give to work and non-work activities.

From the employee perspective, job attributes such as flextime and compressed workweeks are good but not perfect solutions to work/life stress. People who take advantage of flextime or compressed workweeks sometimes find it difficult to disengage from work, increasing rather than decreasing work/non-work conflict[11]. They tend to work longer hours than their counterparts who keep regular office hours[12], increasing the potential for conflict. They are more engaged with their work than workers who keep traditional hours[13], and find it more difficult to disengage from it. The potential for conflict increases when working hours bleed into what would traditionally be considered non-work hours. People who are best able to avoid this conflict are those who strongly identify with their home life or non-work roles, as they are able to create boundaries between their professional and home lives and reduce work/non-work conflict; those who maintain weak boundaries are likely to have higher inter-role conflict[14].

Organizations also stand to benefit from their employees' use of flextime and compressed workweeks. Employees who have the discretion to take the time they need to do the personal things they feel are necessary are less likely to be absent from work than their office-based co-workers[15]. Flexible work schedules have been shown to increase productivity and performance, to increase job satisfaction and, consequently, to lower turnover intentions[16]. One other effect of having the flexibility to leave work for a short time during regular work hours is that employees who have flexible work schedules make more frequent visits to health care providers than office based workers[17]. In the short term, this may cause employers to incur more health care costs but the long term effect may be positive; more research is needed to establish whether or not this is the case.

The benefits of flextime and compressed workweeks are not unqualified. Flextime does not always work well for hourly jobs[18], for jobs that require interaction with coworkers on a real-time basis, for jobs that entail sequenced activity (such as a production line), or for jobs that require coordinated and scheduled activity. In some circumstances, the use of a flextime option by one employee may draw on the resources of colleagues or management to "cover" for the absent employee. Individuals without children have been shown to demonstrate an aversion to family-friendly policies as they can cause unreciprocated transfers of tasks and assignments[19]. Also, depending on whether the organizational culture is one that embraces the use of flextime or merely tolerates it, employees may feel that management may perceive those who take advantage of flextime options as having lower levels of loyalty and commitment to their work and their organization than those who seldom or never use the option[20]. Further, participants in flexible work practices are sometimes viewed as being more absorbed in their caregiving roles than their work activities and so are less likely to advance in their careers than are employees who either did not have children or were not making use of flextime benefits[21].

Flextime benefits are, in general, more often offered to salaried managers and professionals - and especially those who work long hours in the private sector - than to lower ranking or union employees[22]. Also, there is a gender bias in favor of females concerning flextime usage. In general, males who participate in flexible work arrangements are viewed as less likely to succeed than females who use this option[23], but perceptions about the positive and negative effects of the use of flexible work arrangements are part of each organization's unique culture, and the terms of use and acceptability of this benefit may be specific to each organization that employs them.

Telework

Telework is a "work arrangement that allows an employee to perform work, during any part of regular, paid hours, at an approved alternative worksite"[24]. This work can be conducted from any remote location, including a home office, a hotel (e.g., work conducted while on travel), a coffee shop, a telecommuting center, or any other location from which a phone or internet connection can be established. The term "telecommuting" is somewhat more specific. It refers to the regular use of some alternate space outside the traditional central office of the employing firm specifically for the purpose of reducing commuting time. Telework can range from an occasional review of emails while at home or on travel to full time use of a home office or other alternative space.

In 1973, Jack Nilles, with a grant from the National Science Foundation, started a telecommuting program called the "Telecommunications-Transportation Trade-off Project" at the University of Southern California. At the time, computer communications were slow and personal computing equipment was expensive, so telecommuting from a home office was not a workable solution. However, employees could be spared a long commute into a busy downtown office by working at satellite offices which were constructed near to residential communities. These offices had computing and high speed communications equipment that connected them to the central office, enabling workers in information technology professions to accomplish their work without physically being present in the central office. By reducing commuting time, the project was able to increase productivity, decrease turnover, and reduce overhead expenses[25]. As of 2011, 2.3 percent of the American workforce considered their home to be their primary place of work[26], and 24 percent of employed Americans reported that they had spent at least some time working from home[27].

The American adults who spent at least some of their time doing work associated with their employment at some place other than a traditional office were evenly divided by gender and came from all demographic groups and economic strata; their most distinguishing characteristic was that they tended to have higher levels of education than the average worker. People who held multiple jobs were nearly fifty percent more likely to spend some time teleworking than were people who held just one job[28]. This suggests that teleworking is at times used as a coping mechanism – a way of eliminating non-productive time (e.g., commuting) from a schedule or for using some of the time spent at home to complete work tasks.

For the employee, there are several direct and indirect benefits to teleworking: Time that would be spent in commuting is saved, as are the costs of commuting. The expenses of maintaining a wardrobe for office work as well as of eating lunches (and/or other meals) away from home is also reduced[29]. In addition to these, telework has been shown to afford the employee more control over his or her time[30]. With greater flexibility in the scheduling of tasks, teleworkers feel that they are better able to balance work and non-work commitments as well as to better concentrate on their work because, at times, the non-office environment can have fewer distractions than the office environment[31]. Teleworkers have greater feelings of control over their work than their office-based counterparts, have higher levels of job satisfaction and hold more positive views of their own lifestyles[32]. Those who seek teleworking jobs enjoy the autonomy these positions afford and feel that the flexibility of their work improves their ability to perform both work and non-work functions. Teleworkers generally feel that they accomplish more work and non-work tasks than they would have if their time had been more rigidly divided.

There are also several disadvantages to teleworking. Working from a home office can have the effect of blurring the distinction between professional and personal time, and people who work from home are more likely than those who work in an office to dedicate extra time to their jobs[33]. Teleworking also requires more discipline and self-control than office work; while office work has inherent distractions, so too does working at home, especially if there are children or elders in the home who need care. People may also enjoy the social aspects of work – the exchange of ideas, the comradery – and may feel isolation for lack of exposure to the office environment. For those people who are seeking career advancement, some off-hours telework may be a job expectation, but telework that occurs during normal office hours can make an employee less visible to senior management.

Because people who prefer teleworking sometimes do so more for lifestyle reasons than for compensation, an argument has been made that their pay is discounted versus that of comparable office workers[34], namely, that there is a hedonic effect on their wages. Teleworkers in general, however, tend to be more educated and in higher pay brackets than average workers - in part because of their willingness to take work home and spend extra hours on it. Given the wide range of job titles and pay grades of teleworkers, making broad generalizations about the work motivation or the comparative compensation levels of teleworkers versus the office workers may not yield meaningful results.

Organizations also benefit from using teleworking arrangements. Teleworkers can be more effective than office workers for a number of reasons. Teleworkers[35]:

- Tend to work at the times of the day when they will be the most productive.
- Are more likely to finish projects ahead of schedule.
- Work for longer periods of time without interruptions.
- Experience improved communication with the work group.
- Are more available for consultation with clients and supervisors at home by phone than when in the office.
- Are more creative because they concentrate better at home.

In addition, organizations can save between $1,500 and $6,000 per teleworking employee in reduced overhead expenses. First, by not occupying space in an office building, savings result from not having to carry, maintain, and upkeep real estate[36]. (Care should be taken to allocate office overhead expenses only to those employees who actually occupy office space; a per-capita allocation of overhead can misstate department or divisional profitability.) Secondly, employers can recruit workers who do not live within commutable distances from the central office, or hire those who are physically unable to leave their homes, broadening the base from which employees can be drawn, and potentially lowering wage and salary expenses[37]. Additional benefits derive from lower staff turnover, greater flexibility in staffing and hours, and in an increased ability to meet client needs, especially when the clients are located in different time zones[38]. On the other hand, implementing teleworking programs may require an incremental investment in portable communication and computing devices and managers may have to learn new systems and techniques for supervising remote workers[39].

When hiring teleworking staff or extending teleworking capabilities to current employees, management must be able to define work objectives in terms of measurable outputs, to parse work into discrete tasks that can be accomplished without the need for resources that would not generally be available outside the central office. They need to establish communications, metrics and systems that can be used to effectively supervise a remote staff.

Traditional methods of work supervision are time-based, with centralized and hierarchical decision making processes; managing a remote staff is more task-based and requires flexibility and results-oriented goals[40]. Further, as some teleworkers occupy office space on a shared or as-needed basis, office resources also need to be managed and accommodations for teleworkers who are visiting the office need to be made[41].

At present, some 62 percent of organizations in the U.S. report that they encourage employees to telework, but only 7 percent of workers make use of that option[42]. One explanation for this is that only some but not all of the employees within these organizations have been offered the option to telework. Not all jobs are transportable. Further, independent work requires self-control and self-motivation on the part of the employee; some but not all employees are capable of working effectively under these conditions. While rules concerning eligibility for teleworking must be uniform for all employees with the same job functions, an employee's measured performance while teleworking can be used to determine the degree and conditions under which the benefit would be extended to that employee. Not surprisingly, approximately 90 percent of home professionals are self-employed or work as freelancers on a contract basis; only 15 percent of teleworkers were employed by organizations[43].

Teleworking has also been noted for its potential effects on the greater community. A large growth in teleworking could, for example, have the effect of decentralizing the urban structure[44]; it could save time, reduce fossil fuel consumption and relieve traffic congestion[45]. Several local communities have implemented regulations to encourage teleworking. In 1989, four Southern California counties required companies with more than 100 employees at a single location to develop plans for reducing commuter traffic, and similar regulations have been enacted in Arizona, Hawaii, Texas and Washington[46]. The federal government also encourages, where possible, telework for its own employees as outlined in the Telework Enhancement Act of 2010.

Summary

Flextime, telework, compressed work weeks, and other time management options that are designed to give employees more control over their personal schedules have become popular in the U.S. Flextime and teleworking have long been viewed as benefits, but this characterization focuses on how the employee's time is used rather than on what it is that the employee produces. They do not meet the test of being a "form of indirect or non-cash compensation paid to an employee." They are perhaps better viewed as job characteristics – ways of optimizing productivity and promoting cost-effectiveness by providing an employee with enhanced scheduling flexibility. These may be job characteristics that some employees highly desire, but that alone does not qualify them as "work benefits."

The use of flextime, like telework, skews to the upper income, highly educated managers and professionals - employee groups whose work is typically not limited to traditional working hours and who find these options useful in reducing the work/non-work stress that attends to extended hours, travel, and conflicting commitments. The benefits to the organization are clear: It attracts employees who are involved and satisfied, who have low turnover intentions, and are more productive than average workers - characteristics that are important at all levels of the organization, but are especially so among an organization's managers and professionals.

Teleworking and telecommuting have been made much more possible by advances in electronic voice and data communications and yet only a relatively small portion of the working population makes full time use of this job characteristic. This is the case in spite of the potential savings in real estate and office maintenance expenses that organizations stand to gain as well as the savings in commuting (time and expense), clothes, meals and other incidental expenses that would be realized by individuals.

There are two principal reasons for this: One is that many jobs actually require people to be physically present at a work site and so teleworking is not an option. Two is that teleworking is not for everyone. People who telework reported feeling isolated and out of sight of management. They must be capable of self-regulation to a degree not normally required of an office-bound worker. Further, the management of teleworkers differs from that of office-based workers. Projects and tasks must be more detailed and planned and have clearly defined expected results, as teleworkers will be carrying out their tasks and functions more independently than office staff. At the same time, teleworkers can be more focused, creative and results-oriented than office-based workers.

☐

8 CONCLUSION

"Act in such a way that you treat humanity,
whether in your own person or in the person of another,
always at the same time as an end and never simply as a means."

Immanuel Kant
Grounding for the Metaphysics of Morals (1785)

Challenging Old Assumptions about Loyalty and Turnover

The arguments most often given for offering work benefits, namely that they assist in decreasing turnover, in improving job satisfaction and in increasing employee loyalty, sprung from a business environment that cherished stability and security. For some mature industries whose products or services undergo relatively little change over time, these values may still be key. For those other organizations that continually reinvent themselves and their outputs, new and innovative ideas are critical and can translate into reorganization, employee reassignment or turnover, as well as to expansions, mergers, acquisitions, down-sizing or right-sizing. In the sorts of environments where matching human capital to organizational needs changes rapidly, factors that make employees reluctant to turnover can – for some staff - be hindrances rather than advantages. Few organizations operate at either end of this extreme, and so organizations are compelled to strike a balance between the two, selectively retaining or turning over their staff.

For individuals who can continue to contribute knowledge, experience and skills in the face of changing environments, or whose imagination and creativity are the sources of organizational development, retention and loyalty may continue to be a focus of human resource management. Similarly, individuals whose combined knowledge or whose ability to work together can create a competitive advantage for a firm may also constitute a category of individuals whose retention would be a priority. Absent some attribute, knowledge or skill that makes individuals of special value to a firm, however, the arguments to create programs to retain them become less compelling.

Employees may also have expectations about their relationship with an organization, believing, for example, that there is a mutual obligation between them and the organization arising from patterns of behavior and/or personal sacrifices they may have made for the benefit of the firm[1]. Employees may endure periods of low pay, take part time assignments on a temporary basis, develop skills within the organization that are useful only to that organization, work extra hours, forego vacation, etc., on the expectation that the loyalty they exhibit will be returned in kind by the organization[2]. While an employee may have an expectation that an organization will reciprocate for actions taken in excess of what might normally be expected of the employee, in general, these actions create very limited rights on the part of the employee and equally limited obligations on the part of the employer.

Among the myriad of influences on the U.S. economy over the last few decades, two have had the most telling effect on work benefits: the movement towards gender balance in the workplace and the growth of lower end service jobs. A gender balanced workplace is one that needs family-friendly benefits and job characteristics to thrive. In the U.S., neither the government nor organizations support new parents with monetary subsidies and extended leave as well as they do in most other nations. Many firms, however, do offer jobs with flexible working options, an accommodation that is especially helpful for single parents and dual income households.

Concerning the growth of lower end service work in the private sector, these jobs typically have fewer benefits than do manufacturing, professional, or government jobs. As small firm service jobs become the mainstay of people's careers, the lack of leave, retirement, healthcare and family-friendly benefits may make working conditions in the U.S. seem unduly harsh by international standards.

A Summary of Changes in Benefits over the Last Several Decades

Changes made to healthcare and retirement benefits in the last several decades have been directed at cost containment and risk reduction. In both categories, individual employees have been given more responsibility for managing these benefits; health care has become more consumer-directed and saving for retirement more of an individual responsibility than something managed by an organization. While both have resulted in cost-savings for organizations, employees may have also benefitted from these changes. The justification used to rationalize switching from managed care to consumer directed health plans was that opening medical treatments to free market influences would have the effect of fostering competition and improving service. Consumer directed health care does result in lower premiums for most employees as well as lower costs for employers, but it also results in less usage of health care services.

In the 1980s, retirement benefits offered by most organizations switched from defined benefit to defined contribution plans. In doing this, organizations became free of obligations for the long term management of retirement investments. Contributions to retirement plans can be managed year by year and can vary with an organization's profitability or simply with the demands of the labor market. There are advantages for employees as well. In a volatile labor market, it is a help to an employee to not have to stay with a single firm for a "vesting period" in order to have retirement savings begin to accumulate. On the other hand, not all employees have enough of a long term orientation to adequately plan for retirement; nearly half of the adult population nearing a traditional retirement age has not saved adequately for retirement. Social security payments can provide a supplement to other retirement income but are not enough on their own to enable elderly people to retire in comfort. After a century of decline in the number of people aged 65 and over withdrawing from work outside the home, the number of elderly Americans who must continue to work past retirement age has begun to increase.

Paid time off has also undergone changes in recent years. Decades ago, the most common format for time off was to have separate time off allotments for different purposes – for vacation, for holidays and for sick days. More recently, organizations have begun to group these into a single category of time off. The benefit of this for organizations is that sick days, which were called in on short notice, have been reduced. The benefit for employees is increased flexibility in planning the length of periods of time off that can be taken. The U.S., unlike most other countries, has no law or regulation requiring that employers grant paid time off to their employees, and so, only about 60 percent of workers in private industry have access to it. Of these 60 percent, however, approximately 40 percent do not take all of the time off that is due to them, largely because of work pressures.

Unpaid family and medical leave has been available to all full time workers employed by large firms in the U.S. since 1993, when the Family and Medical Leave Act was enacted. The "unpaid" aspect of the leave makes it more accessible to affluent workers than to lower wage earners. The Act was debated in the House and Senate for eight years before it was passed and survived two presidential vetoes before it became law. At the end of this saga, the benefit to which American workers are entitled is less than that they would have in every other nation surveyed by the International Labour Organization, with the exception of New Guinea.

Flexible work options, including flextime, teleworking, compressed work weeks, etc. are widely available to employees whose work is transportable or does not have to be accomplished within a specific set of hours. Schools, manufacturing plants, and shops that are open to the public are examples of places where flexible work options would be difficult to implement; however, where workers can be assigned tasks that can be done without the need for any special equipment or close supervision, or can be planned in detail and accomplished independently with clearly defined results, the option for flexibility becomes much more available. Both the organization and the employee benefit from this. In the case of teleworkers, organizations benefit from not having to provide workspace as well as pay the costs of office maintenance. Employees benefit from not having to commute, have lower food and clothing costs and lower work-life stress. As flexible work options do not involve any cash or non-cash transfers from employer to employee, they cannot easily be characterized as "work benefits." Flexible work options are more accurately described as job characteristics – working circumstances that depict where and when work will be performed.

International Comparisons

From an employee's point of view, work benefits are less frequently available and less robust in the U.S. than they are in all but a very few other countries. The U.S. does not mandate that paid time off be given to employees, or that they be supplied with living wage retirement benefits. As for family and medical leave, the U.S. is virtually alone in guaranteeing unpaid, as opposed to paid, leave for the birth or adoption of a child or for other medical emergencies. Many other countries also award special protections to mothers with minor children, as well as to young and to aged workers.

Congress worked to establish labor rights as part of the "New Deal" of Franklin Roosevelt, and again as a by-product of the wage and price controls instituted during the Second World War to control inflation. Attempts at passing legislation aimed at promoting work-life balance or minimum vacation times have not met with success. Unions are also less pervasive than they had been in the 1950s, and with neither the strength of collective bargaining nor Congressional support, the rate at which benefits are offered to workers has begun to recede. It is in part because low-pay service work from small firms has been the largest portion of job growth in the U.S. over the last four decades, but larger companies are also ceasing to offer benefits as part of a compensation package.

Most other countries view minimum levels of time off, retirement benefits and paid family and medical leave as a form of social protection that constitutes a fundamental part of the rights of their citizens. This concept is articulated in Articles 23 – 25 of the United Nations' Universal Declaration of Human Rights[3], which includes the rights to freely choose employment and to be protected against unemployment, to a living wage, to collective bargaining, to paid time off, to social security, and to security in the event of unemployment, sickness, disability or loss of income in circumstances beyond an individual's control. The Declaration goes on to state that mothers and children are entitled to special care and attention.

In making this statement, the United Nations is not advocating for socialism; there is no statement in the Declaration suggesting that state ownership of business interests is in any way a preferential economic system to capitalism. Rather, the statement advocates for the social protection of citizens, especially for those who would be unable on their own to obtain employment on the minimum terms these stated rights imply.

A Closing Argument for Labor Reform

In the United States, access to paid time off and retirement benefits skews to those in the upper income tiers and to those in professional or managerial positions. The people who have the least access to benefits are those who are in the lower income brackets, those who are in service jobs in the private sector, and especially by those who are engaged in part-time versus full-time work. Access to paid time off, in particular, has declined in the last three decades.

For full time workers, paid time off is available to about 59 percent of the civilian labor force – 71 percent for full time workers and 22 percent for part time workers. Workers in service businesses as well as those in the construction and extraction trades are the most affected by this. About 50 percent of workers in the lowest quartile of earnings have access to paid leave, a number that rises to 83 percent among those in the highest quartile of earnings[4]. Workers in the lowest quartile of earnings were the ones who most frequently cited taking time off (usually unpaid) for illness or medical care and the least likely to take time off for a vacation[5].

The situation for participation in retirement benefits is similar to that of paid time off. For full time workers, retirement benefits are available to 65 percent of private industry workers and 89 percent of workers in state and local governments. Of those working in private industry, 74 percent of full time and 37 percent of part time workers had access to the benefit; for those working for a state or local government, 99 percent of full time workers and 38 percent of part time workers had benefit access. Again, private sector service workers (38 percent) and those in the lowest quartile of earnings (also 38 percent) were the least likely to have access to retirement benefits[6]. One of the outcomes of this is that when compared to other developed nations, the U.S. has one of the highest rates of poverty among its senior citizens.

Before the passage and implementation of the Patient Protection and Affordable Care Act of 2010, the numbers for access to health benefits told the same story. As of 2014, for those in private industry, 69 percent of workers (86 percent of full time and 23 percent of part time workers) had access to health care benefits. For those working for a state or local government, 87 percent of workers (99 percent of full time and 24 percent of part time workers) had access to the benefit. Service workers in private industry (40 percent) were the least likely to have access to health care benefits, as were those in lowest quartile of earnings (34 percent).

The employer share of health care premiums for those who were covered by insurance in private industry was lowest for the low income group (70 percent for an individual employee and 57 percent for family coverage) and highest for the high income group (81 percent for an individual employee and 72 percent for a family)[7]. Under the Patient Protection and Affordable Care Act of 2010, it is workers in the lowest income brackets who will be the ones who will most frequently be required to purchase their own insurance.

Should someone working at a near minimum wage in a coffee shop, perhaps as a permanent job, be able to take a week off with pay every year? Or, if he or she can, make pre-tax contributions to a retirement account that is matched in some ratio by employer contributions? Or receive some corporate or government subsidy when taking time off for the birth or adoption of a child? Or collect some extra financial help for health care? In the U.S., a nation whose guiding principles include a freedom to bargain for terms in an employment contract, the answer is that these are not rights, but privileges that must be earned; these are not entitlements available to every working person. In nations whose guiding principles include providing labor-based social protections for its citizens, the answer is otherwise.

REFERENCES

Chapter 1:

1   Society for Human Resource Management (2014). *2014 Employee benefits: An overview of employee benefits offerings in the U.S..* Alexandria, VA: SHRM

2   U.S. Department of the Army (1995). Ch. 30: The economy and population growth, in Eric Solsten, Ed. , *Germany: A country study.*, Washington, DC: Federal Research Division, Library of Congress

3   U.S. Department of the Army (1995). Ch. 29: Political parties, in Eric Solsten, Ed. , Germany: A country study., Washington, DC: Federal Research Division, Library of Congress

4   U.S. Department of the Army (1995). Ch. 29: Political parties, in Eric Solsten, Ed., Germany: A country study., Washington, DC: Federal Research Division, Library of Congress

5   U.S. History: Pre-Columbian to the New Millenium (2014). *Eugene V. Debs and American Socialism.* Retrieved from: http://www.ushistory. org/us/37e.asp

6   The Socialist Party Platform of 1912 (2013). Retrieved from: http:// sageamericanhistory.net/progressive/docs/SocialistPlat1912.htm

7   Rodgers, D. T. (1978). *The work ethic in industrial America, 1850 – 1920.* Chicago, IL: University of Chicago Press, p. 40.

8   Rodgers, D. T. (1978). *The work ethic in industrial America, 1850 – 1920.* Chicago, IL: University of Chicago Press, p. 40.

9   Rodgers, D. T. (1978). *The work ethic in industrial America, 1850 – 1920.* Chicago, IL: University of Chicago Press, p. 85.

10   Rodgers, D. T. (1978). *The work ethic in industrial America, 1850 – 1920.* Chicago, IL: University of Chicago Press, p. 48.

11   Rodgers, D. T. (1978). *The work ethic in industrial America, 1850 – 1920.* Chicago, IL: University of Chicago Press, pp. 156-159.

12   Espionage Act of 1917 (Act of June 15, 1917), ch. 30, title I, §3, 40 Stat. 219, amended by Act of May 16, 1918, ch. 75, 40 Stat. 553-54, reenacted by Act of Mar. 3, 1921, ch. 136, 41 Stat. 1359, (codified at 18 U.S.C. §2388)

13   Sedition Act of 1918, (1918 Amendments to §3 of The Espionage Act of 1917), Act of May 16, 1918, ch. 75, 40 Stat. 553-54, (repealed by Act of Mar. 3, 1921, ch. 136, 41 Stat. 1359)

14   Palmer, A. M. (February, 1920). The case against the 'Reds'. *The Forum.*

15   Harding, W. G. (December 6, 1921). *First annual message to Congress.* Retrieved from: http://www.presidency.ucsb.edu

16   Rodgers, D. T. (1978). *The work ethic in industrial America, 1850 – 1920.* Chicago, IL: University of Chicago Press, p. 62.

17   Lebergott, S. (1957). Annual estimates of unemployment in the United States, 1900-1954, in *The measurement and behavior of unemployment.* National Bureau of Economic Research, p. 215.

18   Feldmeth, Greg D. (1998). *U.S. history resources.* Retrieved from: http://home.earthlink.net/~gfeldmeth/USHistory.html

19   Grossman, J. (1978). Fair labor standards act of 1938: Maximum struggle for a minimum wage. Department of Labor, Bureau of Labor Statistics, Monthly Labor Review.

20   The Code of Federal Regulations of the United States of America Having General Applicability and Legal Effect in Force June 1, 1938: 1st Ed., Published by the Division of the Federal Register, the National Archives, Pursuant to Section 11 of the Federal Register Act as Amended June 19, 1937, U.S. Government Printing Office, p. 2312.

21   Inland Steel Co. v. NLRB, 170 F. 2d 247 (7th Cir. 1948).

22   Health Insurance Institute 1961, Source Book, p. 10.

23   Taft–Hartley Act, (80 H.R. 3020, Pub.L. 80–101, 61 Stat. 136, enacted June 23, 1947).

24   Domhoff, G. W. (2013). The rise and fall of labor unions in the U.S. from the 1830s until 2012 (but mostly the 1930s – 1980s), Chapter 5. Retrieved from: http://whorulesamerica.net/power/history_of_labor_unions.html

25   Domhoff, G. W. (2013). The rise and fall of labor unions in the U.S. from the 1830s until 2012 (but mostly the 1930s – 1980s), Chapter 7. Retrieved from: http://whorulesamerica.net/power/history_of_labor_unions.html

26   Bureau of Labor Statistics (January 23, 2015). Union Members – 2014. *Economic News Release,* USDL-15-0072

27   Hoeller, P. et al. (2012). Less income inequality and more growth: Are they compatible? Part 1: Mapping income inequality across the OECD. *OECD Economics Department Working Papers No. 924.* OECD Publishing.

28   DeNavas-Walt, C., Proctor, B. & Smith, J. (September, 2012). Income, poverty, and health insurance coverage in the United States: 2011. *Current Population Reports, P60-243*, U.S. Census Bureau.

29   Goldin, C. & Katz, L. (2008). *The race between education and technology.* Cambridge, MA: Harvard University Press.

30   Organisation for Economic Co-operation and Development (2014). *Education at a glance 2014: OECD indicators.* OECD Publishing, p. 143.

31   Organisation for Economic Co-operation and Development (2014). *Education at a glance 2014: OECD indicators.* OECD Publishing, p. 33.

32   Organisation for Economic Co-operation and Development (2014). *Education at a glance 2014: OECD indicators.* OECD Publishing, p. 42.

33   Organisation for Economic Co-operation and Development (2014).

Education at a glance 2014: OECD indicators. OECD Publishing, p. 35.

34 Prescott, E. (2004). Why do Americans work so much more than Europeans? *National Bureau of Economic Research*, Working Paper 10316. Retrieved from: http://www.nber.org/papers/w10316

35 Wharton. (2006). Reluctant vacationers: Why Americans work more, relax less, than Europeans. Retrieved from: http://knowledge.wharton .upenn.edu/article.cfm?articleid=1528.

36 Alesina, A., Di Tella, R., & MacCulloch, R. (2004). Inequality and happiness: Are Europeans and Americans different? *Journal of Public Economics, 88*, 2009–2042.

37 Okulicz-Kozaryn, A. (2011). Europeans work to live and Americans live to work (Who is happy to work more: Americans or Europeans?). *Journal of Happiness Studies, 12*(2), 225-243. doi:10.1007/s10902-010-9188-8

38 Huberman, M., & Minns, C. (2007). The times they are not changin': Days and hours of work in Old and New Worlds, 1870–2000. *Explorations in Economic History, 44*(4), 538-567. doi:10.1016/j.eeh.2007.03.002

39 Cowling, K. (2006). Prosperity, depression and modern capitalism. *Kyklos, 59*(3), 369-381. doi:10.1111/j.1467-6435.2006.00337.x

40 Vespa, J., Lewis, J. & Kreider, R. (2013). America's families and living arrangements: 2012. U.S. Department of Commerce, Economics and Statistics Administration.

41 Toossi, M. (2012). Projections of the labor force to 2050: A visual essay. *Monthly Labor Review, 135*(10), 3 – 16, p.3.

42 Toossi, M. (2012). Projections of the labor force to 2050: A visual essay. Monthly Labor Review, 135(10), 3 – 16, p.7.

43 Harcave, Sidney (1970). *The Russian Revolution.* London: Collier Books.

44 Robert Blobaum, R. (1988). The Revolution of 1905-1907 and the crisis of Polish Catholicism, *Slavic Review, 47*(4), pp. 667–686

Chapter 2:

1 Davis, A. E., & Kalleberg, A. L. (2006). Family-friendly organizations?: Work and family programs in the 1990s. *Work & Occupations, 33*(2), 191-223, p. 214.

2 Davis, A. E., & Kalleberg, A. L. (2006). Family-friendly organizations?: Work and family programs in the 1990s. *Work & Occupations, 33*(2), 191-223, p. 195.

3 Department of Labor, Bureau of Labor Statistics (December 2014). Women in the labor force: A databook, *BLS Reports, #1052*, Table 1.

4 Michel, S. (1999). *Children's interests/mother's rights: The shaping of America's child care policy.* New Haven, CT: Yale University Press, p. 142.

5   Weil, M. W. (1961). An analysis of the factors influencing married women's actual or planned work participation. *American Sociological Review, 26*, 91-96, p. 96.

6   Canady, M. (2003). Building a straight line: Sexuality and social citizenship under the 1944 G. I. Bill. *Journal of American History, 90*, 235-257.

7   Hoffman, L. (1960). Effects of the employment of mothers on parental power relations and the division of household tasks. *Marriage & Family Living, 22*(1), 27-35, p. 31.

8   Hedges, J., & Barnett, J. K. (1972). Working women and the division of household tasks. *Monthly Labor Review, 95*(4), 9-14, p.11.

9   Perry-Jenkins, M., & Folk, K. (1994). Class, couples, and conflict: Effects of the division of labor on assessments of marriage in dual-earner families. *Journal of Marriage & Family, 56*(1), 165-180, p. 177.

10   Barnett, R. C. & Gareis, K. (2006). Role theory perspectives on work and family. In M. Pitt-Catsouphes, E. Kossek & S. Sweet (Eds.), *The work and family handbook: Multi-disciplinary perspectives and approaches* (pp. 209-236). Mahwah, NJ: Lawrence Erlbaum Associates, p. 210.

11   Barnett, R. C. & Gareis, K. (2006). Role theory perspectives on work and family. In M. Pitt-Catsouphes, E. Kossek & S. Sweet (Eds.), *The work and family handbook: Multi-disciplinary perspectives and approaches* (pp. 209-236). Mahwah, NJ: Lawrence Erlbaum Associates, p. 209.

12   Barnett, R. C. & Gareis, K. (2006). Role theory perspectives on work and family. In M. Pitt-Catsouphes, E. Kossek & S. Sweet (Eds.), *The work and family handbook: Multi-disciplinary perspectives and approaches* (pp. 209-236). Mahwah, NJ: Lawrence Erlbaum Associates, p. 209.

13   Weil, M. W. (1961). An analysis of the factors influencing married women's actual or planned work participation. *American Sociological Review, 26*, 91-96. doi:10.2307/2090516eil, 1961

14   U.S. National Center for Education Statistics, *Digest of Education Statistics*, annual, 2010. Census Table 276: College Enrollment of Recent High School Completers: 1970 to 2009.

15   Department of Labor, Bureau of Labor Statistics (December 2014). Women in the labor force: A databook, *BLS Reports*, #1052, p. 1.

16   Grunow, D., Aisenbrey, S., & Evertsson, M. (2011). Motherhood, family policy, education, and careers in Germany, the US, and Sweden. *Kolner Zeitschrift fur Soziologie und Sozialpsychologie, 63*(3), 395-430. doi: 10.1007/s11577-011-0139-0, p. 411.

17   Kossek, E. E., & Friede, A. (2006). The business case: Managerial perspectives on work and the family. In M. Pitt-Catsouphes, E. Kossek & S. Sweet (Eds.), *The work and family handbook: Multi-disciplinary perspectives and approaches*. Mahwah, NJ: Lawrence Erlbaum Associates, p. 617.

18   Pregnancy Discrimination Act, §701(k), 1978.

19   Family and Medical Leave Act, §825.101-b, 1993.

20   Family and Medical Leave Act, §825.113-a, 1993.

21   Dwoskin, L. B., & Squire, M. (2010). FMLA boot camp: Regulatory and case law developments under the Family and Medical Leave Act. *Labor Law Journal, 61*(1), 37-51, pp. 37-39.

22   Scharlach, A., & Grosswald, B. (1997). The Family and Medical Leave Act of 1993. *Social Service Review, 71*(3), 335-359, pp. 335-336.

23   Hunter, L. W. (2000). The adoption of innovative work benefits in service establishments. *International Journal of Human Resource Management, 11*(3), 477-496. doi: 10.1080/095851900339729

24   Ruggiere, Paul John (2000). *Work-family responsiveness in organizations: The influence of resource dependence and institutionalization of program adaption.* Ph.D. dissertation, University of North Texas, United States – Texas, p. 5.

25   Wykoff, Rebecca J. (2000). *Energy, economic and urban impacts of United States postindustrial development: A critique of the postindustrial paradigm.* Ph.D. dissertation, University of Delaware, United States -- Delaware.

26   Davis, G. F. (2009). The rise and fall of finance and the end of the society of organizations. *Academy of Management Perspectives, 23*(3), 27-44. doi:10.5465/AMP.2009.43479262, pp. 29-30.

27   Family and Medical Leave Act, §825.110-a (3), 1993.

28   Davis, G. F. (2009). The rise and fall of finance and the end of the society of organizations. *Academy of Management Perspectives, 23*(3), 27-44. doi:10.5465/AMP.2009.43479262, p. 30.

29   Davis, G. F. (2009). The rise and fall of finance and the end of the society of organizations. *Academy of Management Perspectives, 23*(3), 27-44. doi:10.5465/AMP.2009.43479262, p. 30.

30   Bureau of Labor Statistics (2015). *Labor force statistics from the current population survey*, Series Id: LNS14000000. Seasonally Adjusted Unemployment Rate, Unemployment rate, Age: 16 years and over. Retrieved from: Databases, Tables & Calculators by Subject

31   Lord III, G., & Falk, W. (1982). Hidden income and segmentation: Structural determinants of fringe benefits. *Social Science Quarterly, 63*(2), 208-224, p. 218.

32   Wright, P. M., Dunford, B. B., & Snell, S. A. (2001). Human resources and the resource based view of the firm. *Journal of Management, 27*(6), 701-721, p. 701.

Chapter 3:

1   Wang, M. (2013) Retirement definition. *The Oxford Handbook of Retirement.* New York, NY: Oxford University Press, p. 298.

2 Harvard Business School (n.d.). Local enterprise, the pre-industrial era. *Historical Collections.*

3 United States. National Archives and Records Service. (1974). *Pamphlet Describing M804: Revolutionary War Pension and Bounty-Land-Warrant Application Files.* Washington, D.C.: National Archives and Record Service.

4 Costa, D. (1998). *The evolution of retirement: An American economic history, 1880 – 1990.* Chicago, IL: University of Chicago Press, p. 6.

5 Micklethwait, J., & Wooldridge, A. (2003). *The company: A short history of a revolutionary idea.* New York: Modern Library, p. 58.

6 Hilt, E. (2008). Democratizing incorporation: Law and the industrial enterprise in Massachusetts, 1830-1880. Retrieved from: http://isites.harvard.edu/fs/docs/icb.topic240844.files/hiltpaper.pdf

7 Thoreau, H. D. (1854). *Life without Principle.* Retrieved from: http://thoreau.eserver.org/life1.html

8 Rodgers, D. T. (1974). *The work ethic in industrial America: 1850 – 1920.* Chicago, IL: University of Chicago Press, p. 29.

9 Costa, D. (1998). *The evolution of retirement: An American economic history, 1880 – 1990.* Chicago, IL: University of Chicago Press, p. 197.

10 Seburn, P. (1991). Evolution of employer provided defined benefit pensions. *Monthly Labor Review,* December 1991, 16-23, p. 16.

11 Seburn, P. (1991). Evolution of employer provided defined benefit pensions. *Monthly Labor Review,* December 1991, 16-23, p. 16.

12 Department of Demography, University of California, Berkeley (n.d.) *Life expectancy in the USA, 1900-98.* Retrieved from: http://demog.berkeley.edu/~andrew/1918/figure2.html

13 Revenue Act of 1928, Subtitle B, General Provisions, Part 2, Section 32q.

14 Revenue Act of 1938, Supplement E – Estates and Trusts, Section 165 – Employees' Trusts (a)(2).

15 United States Revenue Act of 1942, Part 1 – Individual and Corporation Income Taxes, Section 162 – Pension Trusts, amending Section 165 – Employees' Trusts.

16 Labor Management Relations Act (Taft-Hartley Act); Section 9, (h).

17 Raymond Dennis, et al., Petitioners, v. United States. 384 U.S. 855 (86 S.Ct. 1840, 16 L.Ed.2d 973)

18 Harry S. Truman: "Veto of the Taft-Hartley Labor Bill.," June 20, 1947. Online by Gerhard Peters and John T. Woolley, *The American Presidency Project.* http://www.presidency.ucsb.edu/ws/?pid=12675.

19 Labor Management Relations Act (Taft-Hartley Act); Section 302, (2)(c) et seq.

20 Chicago Tribune, April 14, 1948 "NLRB Rules Companies Must Bargain With Workers on Pensions" p. 11.

[21] Blakey, G. R. (1963). Welfare and pension plans disclosure act amendments of 1962. *Scholarly Works. Paper 173.* Retrieved from: http://scholarship.law.nd.edu/law_faculty_scholarship/173

[22] See: 29 U.S.C. Sec. 1031(a)(2)(B)(i) (1976).

[23] United States Revenue Act of 1978, Pub.L. 95–600, 92 Stat. 2763, enacted November 6, 1978.

[24] Employee Benefits Research Institute, (n.d.). *Private sector workers participating in an employer based retirement plan, by plan type, 1979-2011.* Retrieved from: http://www.ebri.org/publications/benfaq /index.cfm?fa=retfaq14

[25] Social Security Administration (n.d.). *Age 65 retirement: The German precedent.* Retrieved from: http://www.ssa.gov/history/age65.html

[26] Fenge, R., & Scheubel, B. (2014). Pensions and fertility: Back to the roots. *European Central Bank, Working Paper Series, No. 1734,* p. 9.

[27] Marschalck, P. (1982). The federal republic of Germany with an explanatory hypothesis. In D. Eversley and W. Kollmann, editors, *Population change and social planning,* pp. 62, 87. London: Edward Arnold.

[28] The Social Security Act (Act of August 14, 1935) [H. R. 7260]

[29] The Social Security Act (August 14, 1935) [H. R. 7260], Title II – Federal Old Age Benefits, Part 2 - Old Age Benefit Payments, Sec. 202.

[30] Department of Demography, University of California, Berkeley (n.d.) Life expectancy in the USA, 1900-98. Retrieved from: http://demog.berkeley.edu/~andrew/1918/figure2.html

[31] The Social Security Act (August 14, 1935) [H. R. 7260], Title II – Federal Old Age Benefits, Part 2 - Old Age Benefit Payments, Sec. 202(d).

[32] Social Security Administration (n.d.). Major decisions in the house and senate on social security, 1935 – 2009. *Congressional Research Service Report RL30920.* Retrieved from: www.ssa.gov/policy/docs/ssh/v70n3/v70n3p1.html

[33] Tannahill, B. A. (2013). Social security retirement benefits--the basics. *Journal of Financial Service Professionals, 67*(6), 27-30.

[34] de Grip, A., Fouarge, D., & Montizaan, R. (2013). How sensitive are individual retirement expectations to raising the retirement age?. *De Economist (0013-063X), 161*(3), 225-251. doi:10.1007/s10645-013-9205-5

[35] Blanchett, D. (2012). When to claim social security retirement benefits. *Journal of Personal Finance, 11*(2), 36-87.

[36] Meyer, W., & Reichenstein, W. (2014). Greatly reduced life expectancy: How should it affect a couple's social security claiming strategy?. *Journal of Financial Service Professionals, 68*(1), 39-52.

[37] Cunningham, D. F., & Erickson, P. R. (2009). The "combined

income" tax effect on early versus normal social security benefits for single individuals. *Journal of Financial Service Professionals*, *63*(2), 49-57, p. 57.

[38] Pang, G., & Warshawsky, M. (2014). Retirement savings adequacy of U.S. workers. *Benefits Quarterly*, *30*(1), 29-38.

[39] Poterba, J., Venti, S., & Wise, D. A. (2013). Health, education, and the postretirement evolution of household assets. *Journal of Human Capital*, *7*(4), 297-339.

[40] International Labour Organization (2014). *Social protection for older persons: Key policy trends and statistics*. Geneva: ILO. Table B.4. Non-contributory pension schemes: Main features and indicators.

[41] OECD (2009). *Pensions at a Glance: Retirement-Income Systems in OECD Countries*. United States

[42] United Nations. (n.d.). Universal Declaration of Human Rights, Article 25. Retrieved from: http://www.un.org/en/documents/udhr/index.shtml#a25

[43] International Labour Organization (2014). *Social protection for older persons: Key policy trends and statistics*. Geneva: ILO, p. ix.

Chapter 4:

[1] Iris, S., Diaz, & Wallick, R. (2009). Leisure and illness leave: estimating benefits in combination. *Monthly Labor Review*, *132*(2), 28-34.

[2] Genesis 2:2 NIV

[3] Aristotle, (350 B.C.E.) *Politics*, Book 8, Chapter 3, translated by Benjamin Jowett. Retrieved from: http://classics.mit.edu/Aristotle/politics.8.eight.html

[4] Perrottet, T. (2003). *Route 66 A.D.: On the trail of ancient Roman tourists*. New York, NY: Random House Trade Paperbacks, pp. 66-67.

[5] Husayn Haykal, M. (2008). *The life of Muhammad*. Selangor: Islamic Book Trust. pp. 439–40.

[6] Gaposchkin, M. C. (2013). The place of Jerusalem in Western crusading rites of departure (1095 – 1300). *Catholic Historical Revie*, *99*(1), 1-28, p. 6

[7] Rosenberg, M. (n.d.). Grand tour of Europe: The travels of 17th & 18th century twenty-somethings. Retrieved from: http://geography.about.com/od/historyofgeography/a/grandtour.htm

[8] Aron, C. (1999). *Working at play: A history of vacations in the United States*. New York, NY: Oxford University Press. p. 7.

[9] Aron, C. (1999). *Working at play: A history of vacations in the United States*. New York, NY: Oxford University Press. p. 6.

[10] Aron, C. (1999). *Working at play: A history of vacations in the United States*. New York, NY: Oxford University Press. p. 19.

11   Aron, C. (1999). *Working at play: A history of vacations in the United States.*
      New York, NY: Oxford University Press. pp. 20-22.

12   Rodgers, D. (1974). *The work ethic in industrial America 1850 – 1920.*
      Chicago, IL: The University of Chicago Press. pp. 65, 96.

13   Aron, C. (1999). *Working at play: A history of vacations in the United States.*
      New York, NY: Oxford University Press. pp. 47-48.

14   New York Times (1910, July 31). How long should a man's vacation
      be? President Taft says everyone should have at least three months –
      What big employers of labor and men of affairs think on the subject.
      New York Times Magazine, p. 3.

15   Provisions of French labor laws enacted in June 1936. (n.d.). *Monthly
      Labor Review, 43(*3), 621-624, p. 622.

16   Universal Declaration of Human Rights (1948). United Nations.
      Retrieved from: http://www.un.org/en/documents/udhr/index.shtml

17   Green, F. & Potepan, M. (1988). Vacation time and unionism in the
      U.S. and Europe. *Industrial Relations, 27*(2), 180-194, p. 183.

18   Council of Europe (n.d.). Human rights and rule of law: European
      social charter. Retrieved from: http://www.coe.int/T/DGHL
      /Monitoring/SocialCharter/

19   Directive 2003/88/EC of the European Parliament and of the Council
      of 4 November 2003 concerning certain aspects of the organisation of
      working time. (2003). *Official Journal of the European Union L 299,* 9-17.
      Article 7, p.11.

20   Ghosheh, N. (2013). Working conditions laws report 2012: A global
      review. *International Labour Office.* Geneva: ILO, p. 18.

21   Organisation for Economic Co-operation and Development (2009).
      Special focus: Measuring leisure in OECD countries, *Society at a Glance
      2009: OECD Social Indicators.* Paris, FR: OECD, p. 24, Figure 2.1.

22   Organisation for Economic Co-operation and Development (2009).
      Special focus: Measuring leisure in OECD countries, *Society at a Glance
      2009: OECD Social Indicators.* Paris, FR: OECD, p. 24, Table 2.2.

23   Alderman, L. (November 26, 2014). In France, new review of 35-hour
      workweek. *New York Times.* Retrieved from: http://www.nytimes.com
      /2014/11/27/business/international/france-has-second-thoughts-on-
      its-35-hour-workweek.html?ref=world

24   The Fair Labor Standards Act (FLSA), Overview. (n.d.). Department
      of Labor. Retrieved from: http://www.dol.gov/compliance/laws
      /comp-flsa.htm

25   Strauss-Blasche, G., Ekmekcioglu, C., & Marktl, W. (2000). Does
      vacation enable recuperation? Changes in well-being associated with
      time away from work. *Occupational Medicine, 50*(3), 167-172.

26   GfK Public Affairs & Corporate Communications (2014).
      Overwhelmed America: Why don't we use our earned leave? Retrieved

from: http://www.projecttimeoff.com/sites/projecttimeoff.com/files/reports/OverwhelmedAmerica_FullReport_FINAL.pdf, p. 11.

[27] Avoid the back-to-work blues. (2009). *Journal of Accountancy*, 208(4), 15.

[28] Nawijn, J., De Bloom, J., & Geurts, S. (2013). Pre-vacation time: Blessing or burden?. *Leisure Sciences*, 35(1), 33-44. doi:10.1080/01490400.2013.739875, p. 40.

[29] de Bloom, J., Geurts, S. E., Taris, T. W., Sonnentag, S., de Weerth, C., & Kompier, M. J. (2010). Effects of vacation from work on health and well-being: Lots of fun, quickly gone. *Work & Stress*, 24(2), 196-216. doi:10.1080/02678373.2010.493385, p. 208.

[30] Kühnel, J., & Sonnentag, S. (2011). How long do you benefit from vacation? A closer look at the fade-out of vacation effects. *Journal of Organizational Behavior*, 32(1), 125-143. doi:10.1002/job.699, pp. 137-138.

[31] Nicolao, L., Irwin, J. R., & Goodman, J. K. (2009). Happiness for sale: Do experiential purchases make consumers happier than material purchases?. *Journal of Consumer Research*, 36(2), 188-198, pp. 194-195.

[32] Bureau of Labor Statistics (2014, December 10). Employer costs for employee compensation – September 2014, USDL-14-2208, p. 2. Retrieved from: http://www.bls.gov/news.release/pdf/ecec.pdf

[33] Herda, D. N. (2012). Auditors' relationship with their accounting firm and its effect on burnout, turnover intention, and post-employment citizenship. *Current Issues in Auditing*, 6(2), 13-17. doi:10.2308/ciia-50277

[34] Vales, V. J. (2014). Hawaii government employee unions: How do salary, benefits, and environment affect job satisfaction?. *Organization Development Journal*, 32(3), 41-55, p. 50.

[35] Davis, A. E., & Kalleberg, A. L. (2006). Family-friendly organizations?: Work and family programs in the 1990s. *Work & Occupations*, 33(2), 191-223. Retrieved from: http://www.sagepub.com/journals/Journal200911

[36] Nicholas J. Ketcha Jr., Acting Director, FDIC (August 3, 1995) *FDIC'S Position on the role of vacation policy as an important internal safeguard.* (Letter to: FDIC-Supervised Banks & Savings Banks, All Examiners and State Banking Regulators). Retrieved from: https://www.fdic.gov/news/news/financial/1995/fil9552.html

[37] Community Service in Down Economic Times. (2010). *Journal of Accountancy*, 209(1), 50-54, p. 52.

[38] Martin, J. A., & Adkins Jr., G. E. (2013). Tax practice corner. *Journal of Accountancy*, 215(3), 64-65.

[39] Community Service in Down Economic Times. (2010). *Journal of Accountancy*, 209(1), 50-54, pp. 50-51.

[40] Ford, L. R., & Locke, K. (2002). Paid time off as a vehicle for self-

definition and sensemaking. *Journal of Organizational Behavior*, *23*(4), 489-509. doi:10.1002/job.152, p. 500.

41 Klun, S. (2008). Work-life balance is a cross-generational concern—and a key to retaining high performers at Accenture. *Global Business & Organizational Excellence*, *27*(6), 14-20. doi:10.1002/joe.20229

42 Appelbaum, E., & Golden, L. (2003). The failure to reform the workday. *Challenge (05775132)*, *46*(1), 79-92, p. 79.

43 Hamermesh, D. S. (2014). Not enough time?. *American Economist*, *59*(2), 119-127, pp. 120-122.

44 GfK Public Affairs & Corporate Communications (2014). Overwhelmed America: Why don't we use our earned leave? Retrieved from: http://www.projecttimeoff.com/sites/projecttimeoff.com/files /reports/OverwhelmedAmerica_FullReport_FINAL.pdf, p. 26.

45 World at Work (2010, May). Paid time off programs and practices, p. 2. Retrieved from: http://www.worldatwork.org/adimLink?id=38913

46 Eglash, J. (2003, October 2). Making time. *Human Resource Executive Online*. Retrieved from: http://www.hreonline.com/HRE/

47 World at Work (2014, September). Paid time off programs and practices, p. 26. Retrieved from: http://www.worldatwork.org/ adimLink?id=76002

48 World at Work (2014, September). Paid time off programs and practices, p. 7. Retrieved from: http://www.worldatwork.org/ adimLink?id=76002

Chapter 5:

1 U.S. News and World Report. (November 14, 2014). Health insurance definitions: What the terms mean. Retrieved from: http://health. usnews.com/health-news

2 U.S. News and World Report. (November 14, 2014). Health insurance definitions: What the terms mean. Retrieved from: http://health. usnews.com/health-news

3 From: Fifth Congress. Session 77. 1798. Retrieved from http://history.nih.gov/research/downloads/1StatL605.pdf

4 Murray, John E. 2007. *Origins of American health insurance: A history of industrial sickness funds*. New Haven, CT: Yale University Press.

5 Thomasson, M. (2003). Health Insurance in the United States. *EH.Net Encyclopedia*. Robert Whaples, ed. April 18, 2003.

6 "Chronology of AMA history." Retrieved from: Ama-assn.org.

7 "Chronology of AMA history." Retrieved from: Ama-assn.org.

8 Minor, D. (2010). Kimball, Justin Ford. *Handbook of Texas Online*. Retrieved from: http://www.tshaonline.org/handbook/online /articles/fki09

9   Bärnighausen T., Sauerborn R. (2002). One hundred and eighteen years of the German health insurance system: Are there any lessons for middle- and low-income countries? *Social Science and Medicine 54*(10): 1559-1587.

10 *In sickness and in health: The history of health insurance.* (2009) Retrieved from: http://www.randomhistory.com/2009/03/31_health-insurance.html

11 Wehrle, E. F. (1993). For a healthy America: Labor's struggle for national health insurance, 1943-1949. *Labor's Heritage, 5*(2), 28-45.

12 Scofea, L. (1994). The development and growth of employer-provided health insurance. *Monthly Labor Review, March 1994.*

13 *Source Book of Health Insurance Data, 1981-82.* (1982) Washington: Health Insurance Institute, p. 13.

14 The Stabilization Act of 1942 (Pub.L. 77–729, 56 Stat. 765, enacted October 2, 1942), § 10.

15 *Source Book of Health Insurance Data, 1981-82.* (1982) Washington: Health Insurance Institute, p. 13

16 Internal Revenue Code of 1954, Pub.L. 83–591, 68A Stat. 5, enacted August 16, 1954.

17 *Reinsuring health: Why more middle-class people are uninsured and what government can do.* New York: Russell Sage Foundation Press, June 2006.

18 Smith. J., & Medalia, C. (2014). Health insurance coverage in the United States: 2013. *U.S. Department of Commerce, Economics and Statistics Administration, U.S. Census Bureau.*

19 Smith. J., & Medalia, C. (2014). Health insurance coverage in the United States: 2013. *U.S. Department of Commerce, Economics and Statistics Administration, U.S. Census Bureau.*

20 Smith. J., & Medalia, C. (2014). Health insurance coverage in the United States: 2013. *U.S. Department of Commerce, Economics and Statistics Administration, U.S. Census Bureau.*

21 National health insurance: A brief history of reform efforts in the U.S. (2009) *Kaiser Family Foundation.*

22 Bureau of Labor Statistics, National Compensation Survey, March, 2014. Table 9. *Health care benefits: Access, participation, and take-up rates, civilian workers.*

23 Bureau of Labor Statistics, National Compensation Survey, March, 2014. Table 9. *Health care benefits: Access, participation, and take-up rates, private industry workers.*

24 O'Brien, E. (2003). Employers' benefits from workers' health insurance. *Milbank Quarterly, 81*(1), 5-43.

25 Gaynor, M., Jian, L., & Vogt, W. B. (2007). Substitution, spending offsets, and prescription drug benefit design. *Forum for Health Economics & Policy, 10*(2), 1-31.

26 Fishman, P. A., Ding, V., Hubbard, R., Ludman, E. J., Pabiniak, C., Stewart, C., & ... Simon, G. E. (2012). Impact of deductibles on initiation and continuation of psychotherapy for treatment of depression. *Health Services Research, 47*(4), 1561-1579. doi:10.1111/j.1475-6773.2012.01388.x

27 Brenner, B. K. (2009). Entrepreneurial approach to benefits can improve cost containment and outcomes. *Journal of Financial Service Professionals, 63*(5), 28-31.

28 McWilliams, J. M. (2009). Health consequences of uninsurance among adults in the United States: Recent evidence and implications. *Milbank Quarterly, 87*(2), 443-494. doi:10.1111/j.1468-0009.2009.00564.x

29 McWilliams, J. M. (2009). Health consequences of uninsurance among adults in the United States: Recent evidence and implications. Milbank Quarterly, 87(2), 443-494. doi:10.1111/j.1468-0009.2009.00564.x

30 Nichols, D. R., Plummer, E., & Wempe, W. F. (2011). Equitable taxation and the provision of health insurance subsidies. *Business & Society Review (00453609), 116*(4), 435-466. doi:10.1111/j.1467-8594.2011.00392.x

31 Dworak-Fisher, K., Gittleman, M., & Moehrle, T. (2014). Trends in employment-based health insurance coverage: evidence from the National Compensation Survey. *Monthly Labor Review*, 1-20.

32 Internal Revenue Service. (2015). Affordable care act tax provisions for large employers. Retrieved from: http://www.irs.gov/Affordable-Care-Act/Employers/Affordable-Care-Act-Tax-Provisions-for-Large-Employers

33 Scofea, L. (March, 1994). The development and growth of employer-provided health insurance. *Monthly Labor Review*, 3-10.

34 Cebula, R. J. (2010). The micro-firm health insurance hypothesis. *Applied Economics Letters, 17*(11), 1067-1072. doi:10.1080/00036840902817532

35 Cebula, R. J., McGrath, R. D., & Gubenko, K. (2007). Impact of small businesses on the percentage on the population without health insurance: Exploratory evidence. *Journal of Global Business Issues, 1*(1), 1-8.

36 Stroupe, K. T., Kinney, E. D., & Kniesner, T. J. (2001). Chronic illness and health insurance related job lock. *Journal of Policy Analysis and Management, 20*(3), 525-544.

37 Scofea, L. (March, 1994). The development and growth of employer-provided health insurance. Monthly Labor Review, 3-10.

38 U.S. Department of Health and Human Services (June 28, 2010). "Patient Protection and Affordable Care Act; Requirements for Group Health Plans and Health Insurance Issuers Under the Patient Protection and Affordable Care Act Relating to Preexisting Condition

Exclusions, Lifetime and Annual Limits, Rescissions, and Patient Protections; Final Rule and Proposed Rule". *Federal Register 75* (123): 37187–37241.

[39] Bundorf, M.K. (2012). Consumer-directed health plans: Do they deliver? Retrieved from: http://www.rwjf.org/content/dam/farm/reports/reports/2012/rwjf402405

[40] Domaszewicz, S., Havlin, L., & Connolly, S. (2010). Health care consumerism: Incentives, behavior change and uncertainties. *Benefits Quarterly, 26*(1), 29-33.

[41] Lo Sasso, A. T., Helmchen, L. A., & Kaestner, R. (2010). The effects of consumer-directed health plans on health care spending. *Journal of Risk & Insurance, 77*(1), 85-103. doi:10.1111/j.1539-6975.2009.01346.x

[42] Maillet, P., & Halterman, S. (2004). The consumer-driven approach: Defining and measuring success. *Benefits Quarterly, 20*(2), 7-14.

[43] Gabel, J.R., Lo Sasso, A.T., et al. (2002). Consumer-driven health plans: Are they more than talk now?. *Health Affairs, Supplemental Web Exclusives*. Retrieved from: http://www.ncbi.nlm.nih.gov/pubmed/12703601

[44] Internal Revenue Service (IRS). (July 15, 2002). IRS Revenue Ruling 2002–41 and Notice 2002–45, *Health Reimbursement Arrangements*. Internal Revenue Bulletin No. 2002–28.

[45] Medicare Prescription Drug, Improvement, and Modernization Act of 2003, Public Law 108–173—Dec. 8, 2003 §1201, 26 USC 223.

[46] Blendon, R., Brodie, M., Benson, J., Altman, D., Levitt, L., Hoff, T., & Hugick, L. (1998). Understanding the managed care backlash. *Health Affairs, 17*(4), 80-94.

[47] Barringer, M. W., & Milkovich, G. T. (1996). Employee health insurance decisions in a flexible benefits environment. *Human Resource Management, 35*(3), 293-315.

[48] Dowd, B. E. (2005). Coordinated agency versus autonomous consumers in health services markets. *Health Affairs, 24*(6), 1501-1511. doi:1.1377/hlthaff.24.6.1501

[49] Korobkin, R. (2014). Comparative effectiveness research as choice architecture: The behavioral law and economics solution to the health care cost crisis. *Michigan Law Review, 112*(4), 523-574.

[50] Dixon, A., Greene, J., & Hibbard, J. (2008). Do consumer-directed health Plans drive change in enrollees' health care behavior?. *Health Affairs, 27*(4), 1120-1131. doi:10.1377/hlthaff.27.4.1120

[51] Buchmueller, T. C. (2009). Consumer-oriented health Care reform strategies: A review of the evidence on managed competition and consumer-directed health insurance. *Milbank Quarterly, 87*(4), 820-841. doi:10.1111/j.1468-0009.2009.00580.x

[52] Barringer, M. W., & Milkovich, G. T. (1996). Employee health

insurance decisions in a flexible benefits environment. Human Resource Management, 35(3), 293-315.

53 Lo Sasso, A. T., Helmchen, L. A., & Kaestner, R. (2010). The effects of consumer-directed health plans on health care spending. *Journal of Risk & Insurance, 77*(1), 85-103. doi:10.1111/j.1539-6975.2009.01346.x

54 Domaszewicz, S., Havlin, L., & Connolly, S. (2010). Health care consumerism: Incentives, behavior change and uncertainties. *Benefits Quarterly, 26*(1), 29-33.

55 Dixon, A., Greene, J., & Hibbard, J. (2008). Do consumer-directed health plans drive change in enrollees' health care behavior?. *Health Affairs, 27*(4), 1120-1131. doi:10.1377/hlthaff.27.4.1120

56 Maillet, P., & Halterman, S. (2004). The consumer-driven approach: Defining and measuring success. *Benefits Quarterly, 20*(2), 7-14.

57 French, M. T., Homer, J. F., Klevay, S., Goldman, E., Ullmann, S. G., & Kahn, B. E. (2010). Is the United States ready to embrace concierge medicine?. *Population Health Management, 13*(4), 177-182. doi:10.1089/pop.2009.0052, p. 177.

58 French, M. T., Homer, J. F., Klevay, S., Goldman, E., Ullmann, S. G., & Kahn, B. E. (2010). Is the United States ready to embrace concierge medicine?. Population Health Management, 13(4), 177-182. doi:10.1089/pop.2009.0052, p. 179.

59 Iskarpatyoti, L. (2010). What's next for consumer-directed health plans?. *Benefits Quarterly, 26*(1), 39-42.

60 Domaszewicz, S., & Savan, J. (2014). CDHPs: As enrollment goes up, a time to tune up. *Benefits Quarterly, 30*(3), 19-23.

Chapter 6:

1 Parental and Disability Leave Act of 1985, H.R. 2020, 98th Congress (1985).

2 131 Cong. Rec. D678 (1985) (hearings on the Parental and Disability Leave Act of 1985).

3 Parental and Disability Leave Act of 1986, H.R. 4300, 99th Congress (1986).

4 Parental and Disability Leave Act of 1987, H.R. 925, 100th Congress (1987).

5 Parental and Disability Leave Act of 1987, S. 249, 100th Congress (1987).

6 Parental and Disability Leave Act of 1987, S. 249, 100th Congress (1987).

7 Parental and Medical Leave Act of 1988, S. 2488, 100th Cong. 2nd Sess., (1988).

8 Family and Medical Leave Act, H.R. 770, 101st Congress (1989, 1990).

9   Family and Medical Leave Act, H.R. 770, 101st Congress (1989, 1990).
10 Family and Medical Leave Act, H.R. 770, 101st Congress (1989, 1990).
11 Family and Medical Leave Act, H.R. 770, 101st Congress (1989, 1990).
12 Family and Medical Leave Act, H.R. 770, 101st Congress (1989, 1990).
13 Family and Medical Leave Act, H.R. 2, S. 5, 102nd Congress (1991, 1992).
14 Family and Medical Leave Act, S. 5, 102nd Congress (1991, 1992).
15 Family and Medical Leave Act, H.R. 2, S. 5, 102nd Congress (1992).
16 Family and Medical Leave Act, S. 5, 102nd Congress (1992).
17 Family and Medical Leave Act, H.R. 2, 102nd Congress (1992).
18 Family and Medical Leave Act, H.R. 1, S. 5., 103rd Congress (1993).
19 Family and Medical Leave Act, S. 5, 103rd Congress (1993).
20 Family and Medical Leave Act, S. 5, 103rd Congress (1993).
21 Tysse, G. J., & Japinga, K. L. (1994). The federal family and medical leave act: Easily conceived, difficult birth, enigmatic child. *Creighton Law Review, 28*, 361, p. 363.
22 Mory, M. & Pistilli, L. (2001). The failure of the family and medical leave act: Alternative proposals for contemporary American families. *Hofstra Labor and Employment Law Journal, 18*, 689, p. 695.
23 137 Cong. Rec. S14155, daily ed. Oct. 2, 1991, (statement of Sen. Hatch).
24 145 Cong. Rec. H8536, daily ed. Sept. 22, 1999, (statement of Rep. Woolsey).
25 Mory, M. & Pistilli, L. (2001). The failure of the family and medical leave act: Alternative proposals for contemporary American families. *Hofstra Labor and Employment Law Journal, 18*, 689, p. 695.
26 Smith, B. (2002). Time norms in the workplace: Their exclusionary effect and potential for change. *Columbia Journal of Gender and Law, 11* Colum. J. Gender & L. 271, pp. 284-285.
27 Still, M. (2008). Family responsibilities discrimination and the new institutionalism: The interactive process through which legal and social factors produce institutional change. *Hastings Law Journal, 59*, 1491 (2008), p. 1513.
28 Lenhoff, D. & Withers, C. (1994). Implementation of the family and medical leave act: Toward the family-friendly workplace. *American University Journal of Gender Social Policy and the Law, 3*, 39 (1994), pp. 49-51.
29 Lenhoff, D. & Withers, C. (1994). Implementation of the family and medical leave act: Toward the family-friendly workplace. *American University Journal of Gender Social Policy and the Law, 3*, 39 (1994), p. 41.
30 Title VII of the Civil Rights Act of 1964, SEC. 2000e-2, Section 703.
31 Phillips v. Martin Marietta Corp. 400 U.S. 542, 1971.
32 Alpern, S. L. (2005). Solving work/family conflict by engaging

employers: A legislative approach, *Temple Law Review, 78,* 429, p. 445.

[33] Upton v. JWP Businessland, 682 N.E. 2d 1357, Mass, 1997.

[34] Smith, B. (2002). Time norms in the workplace: Their exclusionary effect and potential for change. *Columbia Journal of Gender and Law, 11* Colum. J. Gender & L. 271, p. 311.

[35] General Electric v. Gilbert, 429 U.S. 125, 1976.

[36] Mory, M. & Pistilli, L. (2001). The failure of the family and medical leave act: Alternative proposals for contemporary American families. *Hofstra Labor and Employment Law Journal, 18,* 689, p. 692.

[37] California Federal Savings & Loan Association v. Guerra, 479 U.S. 272, 1987.

[38] Smith, B. (2002). Time norms in the workplace: Their exclusionary effect and potential for change. *Columbia Journal of Gender and Law, 11* Colum. J. Gender & L. 271, p. 295.

[39] EEOC v. Bloomberg LP, 778 F. Supp. 2d 458 - Dist. Court, SD New York 2011.

[40] EEOC v. Bloomberg LP, 778 F. Supp. 2d 458 - Dist. Court, SD New York 2011, p. 469.

[41] Cari Tuna, C. & Lubin, J. (2009, July 14). Welch: 'No Such Thing as Work-Life Balance'. *Wall Street Journal.* Retrieved from: http://www.wsj.com/articles/SB124726415198325373

[42] EEOC v. Bloomberg LP, 778 F. Supp. 2d 458 - Dist. Court, SD New York 2011, p. 486.

[43] Family and Medical Leave Act of 1993. 29 U.S.C. 2601 et seq. (1993), 29 C.F.R. Part 825, §825.113-a.

[44] Family and Medical Leave Act of 1993. 29 U.S.C. 2601 et seq. (1993), 29 C.F.R. Part 825, §825.101-c.

[45] Family and Medical Leave Act of 1993. 29 U.S.C. 2601 et seq. (1993), 29 C.F.R. Part 825, §825.110-a (1) and (2).

[46] Family and Medical Leave Act of 1993. 29 U.S.C. 2601 et seq. (1993), 29 C.F.R. Part 825, §825.110-a (3).

[47] Family and Medical Leave Act of 1993. 29 U.S.C. 2601 et seq. (1993), 29 C.F.R. Part 825, §825.200-201.

[48] Family and Medical Leave Act of 1993. 29 U.S.C. 2601 et seq. (1993), 29 C.F.R. Part 825, §825.214-215.

[49] Leave Commission Issues Studies on FMLA. (1995). *Labor Law Journal, 46*(11), 713, p. 713.

[50] Cantor, D., Waldfogel, J., Kerwin, J., Wright, M. M., Levin, K., Rauch, J., Hagerty, T., & Kudela, M. S. (2001). *Balancing the needs of families and employers: The family and medical leave surveys, 2000 update.* Washington, D.C.: U.S. Department of Labor, chapter 3.2.2.

[51] Employment Development Department (n.d.). *Paid family leave: About the paid family leave insurance program.* Retrieved from:

http://www.edd.ca.gov/Disability/Paid_Family _Leave.htm

52   International Labour Organization (2014). *Maternity and paternity at work: Law and practice across the world.* Geneva: International Labour Organization, p. 16.

53   International Labour Organization (2010). Maternity at work: A review of national legislation. Findings from the ILO database of conditions of work and employment laws. Retrieved from: http://www.ilo.org/wcmsp5/groups/public/---dgreports/---dcomm/---publ/documents/publication/wcms_124442.pdf, p. v.

54   Family and Medical Leave Act of 1993. 29 U.S.C. 2601 et seq. (1993), 29 C.F.R. Part 825, §825.110-a (1) and (2).

55   Casselman, R., Gundlach, M. J., Morgan, J. F., & Zivnuska, S. (2009). Legally mandated paid sick leave: Response options for businesses and managers. *SAM Advanced Management Journal (07497075), 74*(2), 13-22, p. 13.

56   Baum, II., C. L. (2003). The effects of maternity leave legislation on mothers' labor supply after childbirth. *Southern Education Journal, 69*(4), 772-799, p. 788.

57   Roog, S. A., Knight, L. A., Koob, J. J., & Kraus, M. J. (2004). The utilization and effectiveness of the Family and Medical Leave Act of 1993. *Journal of Health & Social Policy, 18*(4), 39-52. doi: 10.1300/3045v18n04_03, pp. 45-47.

58   International Labour Organization (n.d.). C003 - Maternity Protection Convention, 1919 (No. 3) Convention concerning the Employment of Women before and after Childbirth (Adoption: Washington, 1st ILC session (29 Nov 1919).

59   International Labour Organization (2014). *Maternity and paternity at work: Law and practice across the world.* Geneva: International Labour Organization, p. 1.

Chapter 7:

1   Avery, C. & Zabel, D. (2001). *The flexible workplace: A sourcebook of information and research.* Westport, CT: Quorum Books, p. 5.

2   Martin, V. H. & Hartley, J. (1975). *Hours of work when we choose: The experience of 59 organizations with employee-chosen staggered hours and flextime.* Washington, DC: Washington's Business and Professional Women's Foundation.

3   Society for Human Resource Management (2011). *2011 Employee benefits: Examining employee benefits amidst uncertainty. A research report by the Society for Human Resource Management.* Table 62, p. 47.

4   Casey, P. R., & Grzywacz, J. G. (2008). Employee health and well-being: The role of flexibility and work-family balance. *Psychologist-*

Manager Journal (Taylor & Francis Ltd), 11(1), 31-47. doi:10.1080/10887150801963885, p. 42.

[5] Butler, A. B., Grzywacz, J. G., Ettner, S. L., & Liu, B. (2009). Workplace flexibility, self-reported health, and health care utilization. *Work & Stress, 23*(1), 45-59, p. 53. doi:10.1080/02678370902833932

[6] Thomas, L. T., & Ganster, D. C. (1995). Impact of family supportive work variables on work-family conflict and strain: A control perspective. *Journal of Applied Psychology, 80*, 6-15, p. 11.

[7] Casey, P. R., & Grzywacz, J. G. (2008). Employee health and well-being: The role of flexibility and work-family balance. *Psychologist-Manager Journal (Taylor & Francis Ltd), 11*(1), 31-47. doi:10.1080/10887150801963885, p. 43.

[8] Geurts, S., Beckers, D., Taris, T., Kompier, M., & Smulders, P. (2009). Worktime demands and work-family interference: Does worktime control buffer the adverse effects of high demands?. *Journal of Business Ethics, 84*, 229-241. doi:10.1007/s10551-008-9699-y, p. 236.

[9] Brown, K., Bradley, L., Lingard, H., Townsend, K., & Ling, S. (2010). Working time arrangements and recreation: Making time for weekends when working long hours. *Australian Bulletin of Labour, 36*(2), 194-213, p. 205.

[10] Wirtz, A., Giebel, O., Schomann, C., & Nachreiner, F. (2008). The interference of flexible working times with the utility of time: A predictor of social impairment?. *Chronobiology International: The Journal of Biological & Medical Rhythm Research, 25*(2/3), 249-261. doi:10.1080/07420520802114086, p. 260.

[11] Downes, C., & Koekemoer, E. (2011). Work—life balance policies: Challenges and benefits associated with implementing flexitime. *South African Journal of Human Resource Management, 9*(1), 230-242. doi:10.4102/sajhrm.v9i1.382, p. 236.

[12] Golden, L. (2001). Flexible work schedules: What are we trading off to get them? *Monthly Labor Review – March 2001.* Available at: http://www.bls.gov/opub/mlr/2001/03/art3full.pdf, p. 55.

[13] Pedersen, V. B. & Jeppesen, H. J. (2012). Contagious flexibility? A study on whether schedule flexibility facilitates work-life enrichment. *Scandinavian Journal of Psychology 53*, 347-359, p. 354.

[14] Hecht, T. D., & Allen, N. J. (2009). A longitudinal examination of the work–nonwork boundary strength construct. *Journal of Organizational Behavior, 30*(7), 839-862, p. 853.

[15] Casey, P. R., & Grzywacz, J. G. (2008). Employee health and well-being: The role of flexibility and work-family balance. *Psychologist-Manager Journal (Taylor & Francis Ltd), 11*(1), 31-47. doi:10.1080/10887150801963885, p. 40.

[16] McNall, L. A., Masuda, A. D., & Nicklin, J. M. (2010). Flexible work

arrangements, job satisfaction, and turnover intentions: The mediating role of work-to-family Enrichment. *Journal of Psychology, 144*(1), 61-81, p. 75.

[17] Butler, A. B., Grzywacz, J. G., Ettner, S. L., & Liu, B. (2009). Workplace flexibility, self-reported health, and health care utilization. *Work & Stress, 23*(1), 45-59, p. 54.

[18] Lambert, S. J., Haley-Lock, A., & Henly, J. R. (2012). Schedule flexibility in hourly jobs: unanticipated consequences and promising directions. *Community, Work & Family, 15*(3), 293-315. doi:10.1080/13668803.2012.662803, p. 306.

[19] Almer, E. D., Cohen, J. R., & Single, L. E. (2004). Is it the kids or the schedule?: The incremental effect of families and flexible scheduling on perceived career success. *Journal of Business Ethics, 54*(1), 51-65, p. 53.

[20] Almer, E. D., Cohen, J. R., & Single, L. E. (2004). Is it the kids or the schedule?: The incremental effect of families and flexible scheduling on perceived career success. *Journal of Business Ethics, 54*(1), 51-65, p. 59.

[21] Almer, E. D., Cohen, J. R., & Single, L. E. (2004). Is it the kids or the schedule?: The incremental effect of families and flexible scheduling on perceived career success. *Journal of Business Ethics, 54*(1), 51-65, p. 57.

[22] Golden, L. (2009). Flexible daily work schedules in U.S. jobs: Formal introductions needed?. *Industrial Relations, 48*(1), 27-54. doi:10.1111/j.1468-232X.2008.00544.x, pp. 39-47.

[23] Almer, E. D., Cohen, J. R., & Single, L. E. (2004). Is it the kids or the schedule?: The incremental effect of families and flexible scheduling on perceived career success. *Journal of Business Ethics, 54*(1), 51-65, p. 59.

[24] United States Office of Personnel Management (2011). *Guide to telework in the federal government.* Available at: http://www.telework.gov/guidance_and_legislation/telework _guide/telework_guide.pdf, p. 4.

[25] Mears, J. (2007). Father of telecommuting Jack Nilles says security, managing remote workers remain big hurdles. *NetworkWorld*, p. 27.

[26] Lister, K. & Harnish, T. (2011). *The state of telecommuting in the U.S.: How individuals, business & government benefit.* San Diego, CA: Telework Research Network, p. 9.

[27] Noonan, M., & Glass, J. (2012). The hard truth about telecommuting. *Monthly Labor Review – June 2012.* Available at: www.bls.gov/opub/mlr/2012/06/art3full.pdf, p. 38.

[28] Bureau of Labor Statistics (2014). *American Time Use Survey Summary: Table 6. Employed persons working (1) at home and at their workplace and time spent working at each location by full- and part-time status and sex, jobholding*

status, and educational attainment, 2013 annual averages. Available at: http://www.bls.gov/news.release/atus.nr0.htm

[29] Foegen, J. H. (1993). Telexploitation. *Labor Law Journal, 44*(5), 318-320, p. 319.

[30] Humble, J. E., & Jacobs, S. M. (1995). Benefits of telecommuting for engineers and other high-tech professionals. *Industrial Management, 37*(2), 15.

[31] Jacobs, S. M., & Van Sell, M. (1996). Telecommuting: Issues for the IS manager. *Information Systems Management, 13*(1), 15-19, p. 16.

[32] Young, J. A. (1991). The advantages of telecommuting. *Management Review, 80*(7), 19-21, p. 19.

[33] Foegen, J. H. (1993). Telexploitation. *Labor Law Journal, 44*(5), 318-320, p. 319.

[34] Gariety, B.S. & Shaffer, S. (2007). Wage differentials associated with working at home. *Monthly Labor Review – March 2007.* Retrieved from: http://www.bls.gov/opub/mlr/2007/03/art5full.pdf, Table 2, p. 65.

[35] Jacobs, S. M., & Van Sell, M. (1996). Telecommuting: Issues for the IS manager. *Information Systems Management, 13*(1), 15-19, p. 16.

[36] Flanagan, P. (1993). Here comes the `Road Warriors'. *Management Review, 82*(9), 36-40, p. 38.

[37] Kroll, D. (1984). Telecommuting: A revealing peek inside some of industry's first electronic cottages. Management Review, 73(11), 18-23, p. 18.

[38] O'Leary, M. B., & Cummings, J. N. (2007). The special, temporal, and Configurational characteristic of geographic dispersion in teams. *MIS Quarterly, 31*(3), 433-452, p. 438.

[39] Seaman, M. J. (1997). Telecommuting: A transportation planner's view. *Information Systems Management, 14*(4), 73-75.

[40] Jacobs, S. M., & Van Sell, M. (1996). Telecommuting: Issues for the IS manager. *Information Systems Management, 13*(1), 15-19, pp. 17-18.

[41] Khamkanya, T., & Sloan, B. (2009). Flexible working in Scottish local authority property: Developing a combined resource management strategy. *International Journal of Strategic Property Management, 13*(1), 37-52. doi:10.3846/1648-715X.2009.13.37-52, pp. 38-39.

[42] Khaifa, M., & Davidson, R. (2000). Exploring the telecommuting paradox. *Communications of the ACM, 43*(3), 29-31, p. 29.

[43] Bailyn, L. (1989). Toward the perfect workplace?. Communications of the ACM, 32(4), 460-471, p. 460.

[44] Tayyaran, M. R., & Khan, A. M. (2003). The effects of telecommuting and intelligent transportation systems on urban development. *Journal of Urban Technology, 10*(2), 87-101. doi:10.1080/1063073032000139714, p. 96.

[45] Tayyaran, M. R., & Khan, A. M. (2003). The effects of telecommuting

and intelligent transportation systems on urban development. *Journal of Urban Technology, 10*(2), 87-101. doi:10.1080/1063073032000139714, p. 88.

[46] Jacobs, S. M., & Van Sell, M. (2003). Telecommuting: Issues for the IS manager. In V. Kasacavage (Ed.) *Complete Book of Remote Access: Connectivity and Security* (pp. 307-314). Boca Raton, FL: CRC Press, p. 307.

Chapter 8:

[1] Rousseau, D. M. (1989). Psychological and implied contracts in organizations. *Employee Responsibilities & Rights Journal, 2*(2), 121-139, p. 123.

[2] Rousseau, D. M. (1989). Psychological and implied contracts in organizations. *Employee Responsibilities & Rights Journal, 2*(2), 121-139, p. 128.

[3] Universal Declaration of Human Rights (1948). United Nations. Articles 23-25. Retrieved from: http://www.un.org/en/documents/udhr/index.shtml

[4] Bureau of Labor Statistics (August 16, 2012). Access to and Use of Leave, 2011: data from the American Time Use Survey, Table 1.

[5] Bureau of Labor Statistics (August 16, 2012). Access to and Use of Leave, 2011: data from the American Time Use Survey, Table 2.

[6] Bureau of Labor Statistics (July 25, 2015). Retirement Benefits: Access Participation and Take-Up Rates. *Economic News Release*, USDL-14-1348

[7] Bureau of Labor Statistics (July 25, 2014). Medical Plans: Access Participation and Take-Up Rates. *Economic News Release*, USDL-14-1348

					Increased time off for:		
Country	Vaca-tion [m]	Paid	Hol-idays	Daily Wage Paid [k]	Mo-thers	Young Work-ers	Age/ Years Work -ed
Afghanistan [a]	20	Yes	9	Yes		Yes	
Algeria [a]	30	Yes	9	No			
Angola [a]	22	Yes	15	No			
Antigua and Barbuda [a]	12	Yes	11	Yes			
Argentina [a]	14	Yes	18	Yes		Yes	Yes
Armenia [a]	28	Yes	9	No	Yes	Yes	
Australia [a, d, e]	20	Yes	10	Yes		Yes	
Austria [a]	30	Yes	15	Yes		Yes	Yes
Bahamas [a]	10	Yes	10	No			
Bahrain [a]	21	Yes	8	Yes			Yes
Bangladesh [a, e]	10	Yes	19	Yes		Yes	
Barbados [a]	15	Yes	12	No			Yes
Belgium [a, e]	20	Yes	12	Yes		Yes	
Belize [a]	10	Yes	13	Yes			
Benin [a]	24	Yes	16	Yes			
Bolivia [a, d]	15	Yes	11	No		Yes	
Botswana [a]	15	Yes	11	Yes			
Brazil [a]	30	Yes	12	Yes			
Brunei Darussalam [a]	7	Yes	12	Yes			Yes
Bulgaria [a]	20	Yes	15	No	Yes	Yes	
Burkina Faso [a]	30	Yes	17	No			Yes
Burundi [a]	20	Yes	13	No			
Cambodia [a]	18	Yes	18	Yes			Yes
Cameroon [a]	18	Yes	18	No	Yes	Yes	Yes
Canada [a, d]	10	Yes	10	Yes			Yes
Cape Verde [a]	22	Yes	10	No			
Central African Republic [a]	24	Yes	10	No	Yes		
Chad [a]	24	Yes	12	Yes	Yes	Yes	
Chile [a, d]	15*	Yes	16	No			

Appendix A

Annual Vacations and Holidays with Pay by Country

121

Appendix A - Continued				Increased time off for:		
Country	Vaca-tion [m]	Paid	Hol-idays	Daily Wage Paid [k]	Mo-thers	Young Work-ers	Age/Years Work-ed
China [a]	5	Yes	7	Yes			Yes
Colombia [a]	15	Yes	23	Yes			
Comoros [a]	30	Yes	9	No	Yes		Yes
Congo [a]	26	Yes	10	No			
Congo, D. R. [a]	12	Yes	10	No			Yes
Costa Rica [a]	10	Yes	11	Yes			
Côte d'Ivoire [a]	24	Yes	15	Yes	Yes	Yes	
Croatia [c]	20	Yes	14	Yes		Yes	
Cuba [a]	30	Yes	8	Yes			
Cyprus [a, e]	20	Yes	16	Yes			
Czech Republic [a]	22	Yes	13	No			
Denmark [a]	25	Yes	13	No		Yes	
Djibouti [a]	30	Yes	10	Yes			
Dominica [a]	10	Yes	12	Yes			Yes
Dominican Republic [a]	14	Yes	12	Yes			Yes
Ecuador [a]	15	Yes	15	No		Yes	
Egypt [a]	21	Yes	12	Yes			Yes
El Salvador [a]	15	Yes	12	Yes			
Equatorial Guinea [a]	30	Yes	10	Yes			Yes
Eritrea [a]	14	Yes	16	Yes			Yes
Estonia [a]	28	Yes	12	No	Yes	Yes	
Ethiopia [a]	14	Yes	13	No			Yes
Fiji [a]	10	Yes	10	Yes			
Finland [a]	30	Yes	15	Yes			
France [a, d]	30	Yes	13	No		Yes	
Gabon [a]	24	Yes	13	Yes	Yes	Yes	
Gambia [a]	8	Yes	15	Yes			
Germany [c, d]	20	Yes	11	Yes		Yes	
Ghana [a]	15	Yes	13	No			
Greece [b, d]	20	Yes	14	No			Yes
Grenada [a]	10	Yes	13	Yes			Yes
Guatemala [a, d]	15	Yes	10	No			
Guinea [a]	30	Yes	13	No			
Guinea-Bissau [a]	30	Yes	10	Yes			

Appendix A - Continued				Increased time off for:		
Country	Vaca-tion [m]	Paid	Hol-idays	Daily Wage Paid [k]	Mo-thers	Young Work-ers	Age/ Years Work -ed
Guyana [a]	12	Yes	18	No			
Haiti [a]	13	Yes	18	Yes			
Honduras [a]	10	Yes	12	Yes			Yes
Hungary [c, j]	20	Yes	10	No	Yes	Yes	Yes
Iceland [a]	24	Yes	15	Yes			
India [a, d]	12	Yes	2	No		Yes	
Indonesia [a]	12	Yes	13	No			
Iran, Islamic Republic of [a]	22	Yes	22	No			
Iraq [a, d]	20	Yes	10	Yes		Yes	
Ireland [c]	20	Yes	9	No			
Italy [c, d]	20	Yes	12	Yes		Yes	
Jamaica [a]	10	Yes	10	No			
Japan [a]	10	Yes	15	No			Yes
Jordan [a]	14	Yes	8	No			Yes
Kazakhstan [b]	24	Yes	10	No			
Kenya [a]	21	Yes	10	Yes			
Kiribati [a]	0	No	14	No			
Korea, Republic [a]	15	Yes	12	No			
Kuwait [a]	30	Yes	8	Yes			
Laos [a]	12	No	13	No			
Latvia [b]	20	Yes	13	No		Yes	
Lebanon [a]	15	Yes	20	No		Yes	
Lesotho [a]	12	Yes	11	Yes			
Libya [a]	30	No	11	No			Yes
Lithuania [a]	28	Yes	15	No		Yes	
Luxembourg [c]	25	Yes	12	Yes		Yes	
Macedonia [a]	18	Yes	11	No		Yes	Yes
Madagascar [a]	30	Yes	10	No			
Malawi [a]	15	Yes	14	Yes			
Malaysia [a, d]	8	Yes	13	Yes			Yes
Mali [a]	30	Yes	11	No	Yes	Yes	Yes
Malta [c]	24	Yes	14	Yes			
Mauritania [a]	18	Yes	8	Yes	Yes	Yes	Yes
Mauritius [a]	20	Yes	14	Yes			
Mexico [a]	6	Yes	10	Yes		Yes	Yes

Appendix A - Continued				Increased time off for:		
Country	Vaca-tion [m]	Paid	Hol-idays	Daily Wage Paid [k]	Mo-thers	Young Work-ers	Age/ Years Work -ed
Moldova, Republic of [a]	28	Yes	10	No	Yes	Yes	
Mongolia [a]	15	Yes	6	No			Yes
Morocco [a]	18	Yes	13	No		Yes	
Mozambique [a]	30	Yes	9	No			
Myanmar [a]	10	Yes	15	Yes		Yes	
Namibia [a]	20	Yes	13	No			
Nepal [a]	13	Yes	28	Yes			
Netherlands [c]	20	Yes	11	Yes		Yes	
New Zealand [a]	20	Yes	9	Yes			
Nicaragua [a]	15	Yes	9	Yes			
Niger [a]	30	Yes	12	Yes	Yes	Yes	Yes
Nigeria [a]	6	Yes	11	No	Yes	Yes	
Norway [c]	25	Yes	13	Yes			Yes
Pakistan [a]	14	Yes	10	Yes			
Panama [a]	31	Yes	16	Yes			
Papua New Guinea [a]	14	Yes	11	Yes			
Paraguay [a]	12	Yes	12	No			
Peru [a]	30	Yes	13	Yes			
Philippines [a]	5	Yes	18	Yes			
Poland [a]	20	Yes	13	Yes			Yes
Portugal [a, d]	22	Yes	14	Yes			
Qatar [a]	15	Yes	6	Yes			Yes
Romania [a]	20	Yes	11	No		Yes	
Russian Federation [a]	20	Yes	12	No			
Rwanda [a]	21	Yes	11	Yes		Yes	
Saint Kitts and Nevis [a]	14	Yes	11	No			
San Marino [a]	10	Yes	20	No		Yes	
Sao Tome and Principe [a]	30	Yes	12	Yes			
Saudi Arabia [a, i]	21	Yes	10	Yes			Yes
Sénégal [a]	24	Yes	14	No	Yes		
Serbia [c]	20	Yes	11	No			
Seychelles [a]	21	Yes	13	No			

Appendix A - Continued				Increased time off for:		
Country	Vaca-tion [m]	Paid	Hol-idays	Daily Wage Paid [k]	Mo-thers	Young Work-ers	Age/ Years Work -ed
Singapore [a]	7	Yes	10	Yes			Yes
Slovakia [c]	20	Yes	15	No			Yes
Slovenia [c]	20	Yes	12	No			Yes
Solomon Islands [a]	15	Yes	9	No			
Somalia [a, d]	15	Yes	5	Yes			
South Africa [c]	21	Yes	12	No			
Spain [a, d]	30	Yes	9	Yes			
Sri Lanka [a]	14	Yes	25	Yes			
Sudan [a, h]	20	Yes	11	No			Yes
Swaziland [a]	10	Yes	13	No			
Sweden [c, g]	25	Yes	18	No			
Switzerland [a, d]	20	Yes	8	No		Yes	
Syria [a]	24	Yes	14	Yes		Yes	
Tanzania [a]	28	Yes	17	No			
Thailand [a]	6	Yes	15	No			
Togo [a]	30	Yes	14	No			
Trinidad and Tobago [a]	14	Yes	14	No			
Tunisia [a]	12	Yes	13	No		Yes	Yes
Turkey [a]	14	Yes	8	Yes		Yes	Yes
Uganda [a]	18	Yes	13	No			
United Arab Emirates [a]	30	Yes	13	Yes			
United Kingdom [c, d]	28	Yes	8	No			
United States [c, d]	0	No	10	No			
Uruguay [a]	20	Yes	14	Yes			Yes
Vanuatu [a]	15	Yes	13	No			Yes
Venezuela [a]	15	Yes	12	No			Yes
Vietnam [a, f]	12	Yes	11	Yes			Yes
Yemen [a]	30	Yes	18	Yes		Yes	
Zambia [a]	24	Yes	14	Yes			
Zimbabwe [a]	22	Yes	12	Yes			

Sources: Travail Legal Database, Holidayyear.com.

Notes:

[a] Updated in 2011

[b] Updated in 2009

[c] Updated in 2012

[d] Holidays vary by region

[e] Vacation days vary by type of work done.

[f] Lengths of holidays may vary year to year.

[g] Some additional holidays are half-days only

[h] Varies by community/ethnicity/religion

[i] The law specifies the holidays may be 10 - 15 days

[j] Extra vacation days are awarded for paternity as well as maternity.

[k] Day-wage workers only. A worker who is paid on a daily basis and who works on the working day before and the working day after a public holiday will be paid for the public holiday or given an alternate day off.

[l] Where a "one month" vacation is specified, the number of days is calculated at 22.

[m] Based on a five day work week.

Appendix B
Maternity Leave Around the World

Country	Length of Leave	Percent of Wages	Who Pays?
Afghanistan	90 days	100	Employer
Algeria	14 weeks	100	Social Security
Angola	90 days	100	Employer
Antigua/Barbuda	13 weeks	60	S.S. and possible employer supplement
Argentina	90 days	100	Social Security
Australia***	18 weeks	Nat. min.	Social Security
Austria	16 weeks	100	Social Security
Bahamas	8 weeks	100	40% Employer / 60% S.S.
Bahrain	45 days	100	Employer
Bangladesh	12 weeks	100	Employer
Barbados	12 weeks	100	Social Security
Belarus	126 days	100	Social Security
Belgium	15 weeks	82 for 30 days, 75%* thereafter	Social Security
Belize	12 weeks	80	Social Security
Benin	14 weeks	100	Social Security
Bolivia	60 days	100 of nat'l minimum wage + 70% of wages above minimum wage	Social Security
Botswana	12 weeks	25	Employer
Brazil	120 days	100	Social Security
Bulgaria	120-180 days	100	Social Security
Burkina Faso	14 weeks	100	S.S. & Employer
Burundi	12 weeks	50	Employer
Cambodia	90 days	50	Employer
Cameroon	14 weeks	100	Social Security
Canada	17-18 weeks	55 for 15 weeks	Unemployment Insurance
Cent. African Rep.	14 weeks	50	Social Security

Country	Length of Leave	Percent of Wages	Who Pays?
Chad	14 weeks	50	Social Security
Chile	18 weeks	100	Social Security
China	90 days	100	Employer
Colombia	12 weeks	100	Social Security
Comoros	14 weeks	100	Employer
Congo	15 weeks	100	50% Employer / 50% S.S.
Costa Rica	4 months	100	50% Employer / 50% S.S.
Côte d'Ivoire	14 weeks	100	Social Security
Cuba	18 weeks	100	Social Security
Cyprus	16 weeks	75	Social Security
Dem. Rep. of the Congo	14 weeks	67	Employer
Denmark	18 weeks	100* 10 more weeks may be taken by either parent	Social Security
Djibouti	14 weeks	50 (100% for public employees)	Employer / S.S.
Dominica	12 weeks	60	S.S. / Employer
Dominican Republic	12 weeks	100	50% Employer / 50% S.S.
Ecuador	12 weeks	100	25% Employer / 75% S.S.
Egypt	50 days	100	S.S. / Employer
El Salvador	12 weeks	75	Social Security
Equatorial Guinea	12 weeks	75	Social Security
Ethiopia	90 days	100	Employer
Fiji	84 days	Flat rate	Employer
Finland	105 days	80	Social Security
France	16-26 weeks	100	Social Security
Gabon	14 weeks	100	Social Security
Germany	14 weeks	100	S.S.to ceiling; employer pays difference
Ghana	12 weeks	50	Employer
Greece	16 weeks	75	Social Security
Grenada	3 months	100 (2 months), 60% for 3rd month	S.S. / Employer

Country	Length of Leave	Percent of Wages	Who Pays?
Guatemala	12 weeks	100	33% Employer / 67% S.S.
Guinea	14 weeks	100	50% Employer / 50% S.S.
Guinea-Bissau	60 days	100	Employer / S.S.
Guyana	13 weeks	70	Social Security
Haiti	12 weeks	100 for 6 weeks	Employer
Honduras	10 weeks	100 for 84 days	33% Employer / 67% S.S.
Hungary	24 weeks	100	Social Security
Iceland	2 months	Flat rate	Social Security
India	12 weeks	100	Employer / S.S.
Indonesia	3 months	100	Employer
Iran	90 days	66.7 for 16 weeks	Social Security
Iraq	62 days	100	Social Security
Ireland	14 weeks	70* or fixed rate	Social Security
Israel	12 weeks	75*	Social Security
Italy	5 months	80	Social Security
Jamaica	12 weeks	100 for 8 weeks	Employer
Japan	14 weeks	60	Social Security or health insurance
Jordan	10 weeks	100	Employer
Kenya	2 months	100	Employer
Korea, Republic of	60 days	100	Employer
Kuwait	70 days	100	Employer
Laos	90 days	100	Social Security
Lebanon	40 days	100	Employer
Lesotho***	12 weeks	2 weeks	Employer
Libyan Arab Jamahiriya	50 days	50	Employer
Liechtenstein	8 weeks	80	Social Security
Luxembourg	16 weeks	100*	Social Security
Madagascar	14 weeks	100	50% Employer / 50% S.S.
Malaysia	60 days	100	Employer
Mali	14 weeks	100	Social Security
Malta	13 weeks	100	Social Security

Country	Length of Leave	Percent of Wages	Who Pays?
Mauritania	14 weeks	100	Social Security
Mauritius	12 weeks	100	Employer
Mexico	12 weeks	100	Social Security
Mongolia	101 days		
Morocco	12 weeks	100	Social Security
Mozambique	60 days	100	Employer
Myanmar	12 weeks	66.7	Social Security
Namibia	12 weeks	as prescribed	Social Security
Nepal	52 days	100	Employer
Netherlands	16 weeks	100	Social Security
New Zealand	14 weeks	0	
Nicaragua	12 weeks	60	Social Security
Niger	14 weeks	50	Social Security
Nigeria	12 weeks	50	Employer
Norway	18 weeks	100, and 26 extra paid weeks by either parent	Social Security
Pakistan	12 weeks	100	Employer
Panama	14 weeks	100	Social Security
Papua New Guinea	6 weeks	0	
Paraguay	12 weeks	50 for 9 weeks	Social Security
Peru	90 days	100	Social Security
Philippines	60 days	100	Social Security
Poland	16-18 weeks	100	Social Security
Portugal	98 days	100	Social Security
Qatar	40-60 days	100 for civil servants	Agency concerned
Romania	112 days	50-94	Social Security
Russia	140 days	100	Social Security
Rwanda	12 weeks	67	Employer
Saint Lucia	13 weeks	65	Social Security
Sao Tome/Principe	70 days	100 for 60 days	Social Security
Saudi Arabia	10 weeks	50 or 100	Employer
Senegal	14 weeks	100	Social Security
Seychelles	14 weeks	flat rate for 10 weeks	Social Security

Country	Length of Leave	Percent of Wages	Who Pays?
Singapore	8 weeks	100	Employer
Solomon Islands	12 weeks	25	Employer
Somalia	14 weeks	50	Employer
South Africa	12 weeks	45	Unemployment Insurance
Spain	16 weeks	100	Social Security
Sri Lanka	12 weeks	100	Employer
Sudan	8 weeks	100	Employer
Swaziland***	12 weeks	2 weeks	Employer
Sweden	14 weeks	450 days paid parental leave: 75%, 360 days; 90 days, flat rate	Social Security
Switzerland	8 weeks	100	Employer
Syria	75 days	100	Employer
Tanzania	12 weeks	100	Employer
Thailand	90 days	100 for 45 days; 50% for next 15 days	Employer for 45 days, then Social Security
The Gambia	12 weeks	100	Employer
Togo	14 weeks	100	50% Employer / 50% S.S.
Trinidad/Tobago	13 weeks	60-100	S.S./Employer
Tunisia	30 days	67	Social Security
Turkey	12 weeks	66.7	Social Security
Uganda	8 weeks	100 for one month	Employer
Ukraine	126 days	100	Social Security
United Arab Emirates	45 days	100	Employer
United Kingdom	14-18 weeks	90 for 6 weeks, flat rate after	Social Security
United States	12 weeks	0	
Uruguay	12 weeks	100	Social Security
Venezuela	18 weeks	100	Social Security
Viet Nam	4-6 months	100	Social Security
Yemen	60 days	100	Employer
Zambia	12 weeks	100	Employer
Zimbabwe	90 days	60/75	Employer

* up to a ceiling
** voluntary insurance available
*** Updated 2011.
Source: International Labour Organization, 1998.
Note: As of 2015, only Lesotho, Swaziland, Papua New Guinea and the United States did not provide paid maternity leave.

ABOUT THE AUTHOR

Dr. Robert Klonoski is an Associate Professor of Business Administration at Mary Baldwin College in Virginia, USA. He worked in the financial services industry and as an entrepreneur. Professor Klonoski holds a B.S. in Finance from Fairfield University, an M.B.A. from the University of Connecticut, a J.D. from Brooklyn Law School and a Doctorate in Management from the University of Maryland, University College.

www.ingramcontent.com/pod-product-compliance
Lightning Source LLC
Chambersburg PA
CBHW051921170526
45168CB00001B/492